Balance-of-Payments Policy

B. J. Cohen

D0068489

Penguin Books

Penguin Books Ltd, Harmondsworth,
Middlesex, England
Penguin Books Inc., 7110 Ambassador Road,
Baltimore, Md. 21207, U.S.A.
Penguin Books Australia Ltd, Ringwood,
Victoria, Australia

First published by Penguin Books Ltd. 1969
First published by Penguin Books Inc 1970
Reprinted 1972, 1974
Copyright © B. J. Cohen, 1969

Printed in the United States of America by
Universal Lithographers, Inc.
Set in Linotype Times

M.R. Myler

Penguin Education

Penguin Modern Economics Texts
General Editor: B. J. McCormick

International Trade
Editor: J. Spraos

Balance-of-Payments Policy
B. J. Cohen

(c) 1969

Penguin Modern Economics Texts

This volume is one in a series of unit texts designed to reduce the price of knowledge for students of economics in universities and colleges of higher education. The units may be used singly or in combination with other units to form attractive and unusual teaching programmes. The volumes will cover the major teaching areas but they will differ from conventional books in their attempt to chart and explore new directions in economic thinking. The traditional divisions of theory and applied, of positive and normative and of micro and macro will tend to be blurred as authors impose new and arresting ideas on the traditional corpus of economics. Some units will fall into conventional patterns of thought but many will transgress established beliefs.

Penguin Modern Economics Texts are published in units in order to achieve certain objectives. First, a large range of short texts at inexpensive prices gives the teacher flexibility in planning his course and recommending texts for it. Secondly, the pace at which important new work is published requires the project to be adaptable. Our plan allows a unit to be revised or a fresh unit to be added with maximum speed and minimal cost to the reader.

The international range of authorship will, it is hoped, bring out the richness and diversity in economic analysis and thinking.

B.J.McC.

For Dido

Contents

Editorial Foreword

This textbook is one of many which will attempt to cover between them the main sub-areas of International Economics. Two, including the present one, appear in the initial batch of *Penguin Modern Economics Texts*. The others will follow in fairly quick succession.

International Economics is the oldest branch of Economics viewed as a discipline and the second oldest (after Public Finance) viewed as an area of practical concern for a national economy. The earliest extant account of England's balance of trade goes back to 1355! It hardly needs saying, however, that it is not for antiquarian reasons that International Economics commands attention at the present time. Any alert citizen knows that some of the most pressing and frequently the most intractable economic problems are international in character.

The management of the balance of payments, with which this volume is concerned, lies right at the heart of problems that attract wide public interest. This poses a challenge for the author. He must remain detached from the ephemeral, day-to-day crises and alarms which preoccupy politicians and journalists, yet must be attuned to problems of immediate relevance. Professor Cohen responds to this challenge in an interesting and stimulating fashion.

J.S.

Preface

The primary purpose of this book is to demonstrate that the subject of balance-of-payments policy can be comprehended readily by any student familiar with the basic principles of economic theory. Balance-of-payments policy is merely a sub-set of national economic policy in general, and therefore shares most of the same means and ends. The instruments of balance-of-payments policy are precisely the same as the instruments of national economic policy in general. They include the government's policies in the fields of money and banking, debt management, government expenditure and taxation, as well as its policies in the fields of international trade and investment. All of these influence the balance of payments (though it is true of course that the external incidence of many may be quite marginal to their domestic impact). All are part of the arsenal of weapons available to the authorities responsible for dealing with problems of foreign imbalance and adjustment.

Likewise, the authorities responsible for national balance-of-payments policy are precisely the same financial authorities who are responsible for national economic policy in general. They are the officials of the national Treasury and central bank. The balance of external payments and receipts is just one of their several concerns. And, similarly, the rationale for balance-of-payments policy is just the same rationale as that for national economic policy in general – namely, to maximize the welfare of the country's citizens. A government intervenes in the economic life of the nation in order to promote an efficient allocation of resources and to influence the distribution of income, to maintain stability of prices and employment and to encourage a steady growth of output. Policies aimed directly at affecting the balance of payments are no less concerned with these objectives than policies that are ostensibly domestic in orientation.

From all of this it follows that balance-of-payments policy shares with national economic policy the same fundamental problem as confronts every economic decision maker – the problem of choice. Walter Heller, former chairman of the U.S. Council of Economic Advisers under Presidents Kennedy and Johnson, has written of the political economist:

Problems of choice are his meat and drink. His method is to factor out the costs, the benefits, and the net advantage or disadvantage of alternative courses of action (Heller, 1967, p. 5).

These words summarize the theme of this book.

The book is divided into four chapters. We begin in chapter 1 with an analysis of the three concepts of the 'balance of payments'. Chapter 2, in turn, considers the foreign-exchange market, which is the main arena of balance-of-payments policy. Chapter 3 is the heart of the book. Here we concentrate on the theory of balance-of-payments policy, identifying the range of policy instruments available to the authorities and discussing the various factors influencing the choice among policy alternatives. Finally, chapter 4 examines balance-of-payments policy as it was actually practised by several major countries in recent years.

This book has benefited greatly from the comments and suggestions, and most of all from the wisdom, of a number of my colleagues. It is a pleasure to acknowledge their aid. I am particularly indebted to Professor John Spraos of University College, London, editor of this series, for his guidance and encouragement. In addition, I wish to acknowledge my deep gratitude to the following students and practitioners of balance-of-payments policy, all of whom contributed above and beyond the call of duty in critically evaluating early drafts of various chapters: Professors Stanley W. Black, Anthony M. J. Lanyi, Fritz Machlup and

Burton G. Malkiel of Princeton University, Professor Peter B. Kenen of Columbia University, and Mr George Bossy and Mr Scott E. Pardee of the Federal Reserve Bank of New York. Needless to say, any remaining faults these chapters may contain are my responsibility alone. Finally, I owe sincere thanks to my thorough and energetic research assistant, Mr J. Edward Jones III.

1 The Balance of Payments

The term balance of payments is an ambiguous one. It is usually used loosely without any precise definition of what it is intended to describe. As a result, debates on balance-of-payments policy are often unnecessarily confused. It is appropriate for our survey to begin, therefore, with a discussion of the various possible meanings of the term.

Three fundamentally different ideas are continually called by the same name. What is indiscriminately called the balance of payments may be (1) an *accounting balance*, i.e. a balance of credits and debits; or (2) a *programme balance*, i.e. a balance of needs and desires; or (3) a *market balance*, i.e. a balance of supply and demand (Machlup, 1950). All three of these concepts are closely related, and they all figure directly in the making of balance-of-payments policy. For the purpose of analytical clarity, each will be discussed separately.

The Accounting Balance

The accounting balance of payments of a country is a systematic record of all economic transactions between the residents of a country and foreign residents. For any specified period of time (most conveniently a year), the statistical record shows the character and dimensions of the country's international economic relationships with the rest of the world. It shows the country's trading position, changes in its net position as foreign lender or borrower, and changes in its official reserve holdings. For these reasons it can be very useful to the financial authorities of the nation.

Double-entry book-keeping

The accounting balance of payments is constructed according to the principles of double-entry book-keeping. Every economic transaction has two sides, a debit and a credit. Both sides must be recorded, credits being represented by a plus (+) sign, or no sign at all, debits being represented by a minus (−) sign. To the student these principles may seem confusing at first. However, the basic rule for recording entries is really quite simple. Any transaction giving rise to a receipt from the rest of the world, increasing net claims on foreigners, is recorded as a credit in the accounting balance. The receipt itself either may take the form of a rise of residents' foreign assets or balances of foreign currencies; or it may take the form of a decline of foreign liabilities or of foreign balances of local currency: whatever its form, the receipt is recorded as a debit. Conversely, any transaction giving rise to a payment to the rest of the world, increasing net liabilities to foreigners, is recorded in the accounting balance as a debit; the payment is recorded as a credit.

For example, consider the balance of payments of an imaginary country called Cohenia, and suppose that a Cohenian corporation ships a certain amount of exports in the course of a year. In the Cohenian balance of payments the exports will appear as a credit entry because they give rise to receipts from abroad. The receipts themselves will appear as a debit entry, and this is so whether they are in foreign currency or in local currency; in either case, they represent an increase of net Cohenian claims on foreigners.

Credits (+)	*Debits* (−)
Exports	Increase of net claims on foreigners (receipts from exports)

Likewise, such items as foreign tourist expenditure in Cohenia, foreign spending on Cohenian shipping or airlines, and foreign purchases of Cohenian insurance are all entered as credits in the balance of payments. Being sales of Cohenian services, they all give rise to receipts from abroad. These receipts, which increase net Cohenian claims on foreigners, are themselves recorded as debits.

Credits (+)	*Debits* (−)
Sales of services	Increase of net claims on foreigners (receipts from sales of services)

By the same token, Cohenian imports of foreign goods and services will appear as debits in the accounting balance, while the corresponding payments to the rest of the world are entered as credits.

Credits (+)	*Debits* (−)
Increase of net liabilities to foreigners (payments for imports)	Imports of goods and services

Unilateral transfers similarly appear twice in the balance of payments, despite the fact that they are actually one-sided transactions lacking a *quid pro quo*. A person or government transfers commodities, services or money to some other person or government, but receives nothing in exchange. Yet in any system of accounts all transactions must be 'accounted for'. If any items are given away, that fact must be recorded; the *quid pro quo* must be supplied. The method for doing so is to make an entry indicating the character of the gift on the side of the account opposite to the entry for the item given or received. This not only 'accounts for' the gift, but also preserves balance in the accounts. Thus, for instance, when an immigrant remits part of his earnings to 'the old country', the net change in claims on foreigners, the primary entry, is recorded as a credit.

But at the same time a debit is entered listing the unilateral transfer, usually as a 'private remittance'. This is the statistical *quid pro quo*, the analogue to the import item listed when payment is made for a foreign commodity or service.

Credits (+)	Debits (−)
Increase of net liabilities to foreigners (transfer payment)	Private remittance

Similarly, a debit is entered listing each government grant as the accounting counterpart of the credit recording a transfer payment either 'in kind' (export of goods or services) or 'in cash' (remittance of cash or a financial claim).

Credits (+)	Debits (−)
Export of goods or services (transfer payment in kind)	Government grant

Credits (+)	Debits (−)
Increase of net liabilities to foreigners (transfer payment in cash)	Government grant

Financial transactions, such as the purchases and sales of foreign assets and borrowing from and lending to foreigners, also appear on both the credit and debit sides of the accounting balance. International investments may be entered as 'direct' investments if they involve an outright extension of domestic enterprise abroad through the purchase of a permanent interest in a foreign company or through the establishment of a new foreign facility. If, however, they involve a loan or a purchase of securities issued by foreign-controlled firms, they are entered as 'portfolio' investments. When an investor at home acquires an earning asset abroad, a payment is made to foreigners.

The payment is therefore recorded as a credit, while the investment itself is listed as a debit; and the same rule applies whenever a financial liability abroad is liquidated. Conversely, any financial transaction which adds to foreign liabilities or reduces foreign assets is listed as a credit, with the corresponding payment appearing as a debit.

Credits (+)	*Debits* (−)
Increase of net liabilities to foreigners (payments for net investments)	Net external investment by residents (acquisition of earning assets abroad; or liquidation of liabilities)

Credits (+)	*Debits* (−)
Net internal investment by foreigners (acquisition of earning assets locally; or liquidation of liabilities)	Increase of net claims on foreigners (receipts from net investments)

Finally, a sale of gold by the central authorities is recorded as a credit, with the corresponding receipt entered as a debit. And the same rule applies to a sale of any other reserve asset held by the authorities.

Credits (+)	*Debits* (−)
Official sale of gold or other reserve assets	Increase of net claims on foreigners (receipts from sale of gold or other reserve assets)

Current account and capital account

The balance of payments is not only divided vertically into credits and debits according to the principles of double-entry book-keeping. It is also divided horizontally into two major categories according to the broad nature of the transactions concerned and their relationship to the national economy. These categories are the current account and the capital account.

The *current account* consists of all transactions relating to the reporting country's current national income and current expenditures. These include exports and imports of goods and services along with, as we shall see, unilateral transfers. These are 'current' transactions: they give rise to or are a use of current national income. They are distinguished from transactions in financial assets – 'capital' transactions – which directly affect wealth and debt, hence national income in future periods but not national income produced or consumed currently. When a Cohenian investor makes a portfolio investment abroad, purchasing foreign securities or lending abroad, he acquires a foreign asset – a claim on foreigners – which will earn income in the future. In the current period, however, national income is not affected directly by the transaction; only the creditor-debtor position of Cohenia is altered by the exchange of one type of financial asset for another.[1] By analogy, the same holds true when a Cohenian corporation makes a direct investment abroad. Short-term liabilities (say, currency or demand deposits) are exchanged for an equity asset, and while the international creditor–debtor position of Cohenia is directly affected, its current income is not. All such private or official transactions affecting the international investment position of a country rather than its current income are segregated from the current account and grouped instead in the *capital account* of the balance of payments. The capital account also includes all official reserve transactions (since these too affect the country's international investment position).

The following schedule lists the types of transactions usually distinguished in the current account of the balance of payments:

---

1. The reader should be aware that while national income is not affected directly it is affected indirectly in an opportunity-cost sense – that is, in the sense that instead of investing abroad the investor might alternatively have invested or consumed at home.

(1) Merchandise imports and exports.

(2) Transportation (freight and merchandise insurance).

(3) Travel (goods and services, including transportation, purchased outside the country of residence).

(4) Investment income (interest, dividends and profits on securities or property owned outside the country of residence).

(5) Other services (insurance, royalties, commissions, fees and government transactions not recorded elsewhere).

(6) Private transfers (personal and institutional remittances).

(7) Official transfers (pensions, reparations, and grants).

Included in the capital account are the following types of transactions:

(1) Direct investment (transactions involving a permanent interest in enterprise outside the country of residence).

(2) Portfolio investment (transactions in assets and liabilities outside the country of residence with an original maturity of more than twelve months).

(3) Short-term investment (transactions in assets and liabilities outside the country of residence with an original maturity of twelve months or less).

(4) Government capital (official transactions in assets and liabilities outside the country of residence, excluding reserve assets).

(5) Official reserve transactions (changes in the reporting country's monetary gold stock, holdings of convertible

foreign currencies and net position in the International Monetary Fund; and for reserve-currency countries, changes in liquid foreign liabilities).

As an illustration, it may be instructive to examine the balance of payments of one or two real countries in some detail. Tables 1a and 1b present the payments accounts respectively of the United States and of the United Kingdom for the year 1966. Credits are indicated by a plus sign, debits by a minus sign. All reported transactions are allocated to either the current account or the capital account.

In the current account, by far the most important item is merchandise, or visible trade. This is the oldest and still the most basic form of economic relationship between nations. Commodities not produced at home or produced only at relatively high cost are imported, and in exchange commodities that can be produced relatively inexpensively at home are exported. For any one nation, the difference between merchandise exports and imports (credits and debits) is called the balance of trade, and this is usually watched by the financial authorities almost as closely as the balance-of-payments as a whole. Most people regard the balance of trade as 'favourable' when exports exceed imports, and as 'unfavourable' when imports exceed exports. That this should be so is a testament to the durability of mercantilist thinking, which traditionally places the greatest stress on an earned foreign surplus as the most direct means to national wealth.

Economists long ago exposed the fallacy of mercantilist thought: the real gains from trade are to be found in the cheaper imports made available for home consumption, not in expanded export sales. But even within the mercantilist way of looking at things this view of the balance of trade seems misguided, for it obviously ignores the presence of the other items in the current account. In fact, a marked excess of merchandise imports over exports may be quite consistent with a total current-account balance or even surplus if the country happens to be a large net seller of ser-

Table 1a
United States Balance of Payments, 1966, in billions of dollars (U.S. Department of Commerce, Office of Business Economics)

Current Account		+2·2
Exports of goods and services		+43·0
Merchandise		+29·2
Services		+13·8
Transportation	+2·6	
Travel	+1·6	
Income on U.S. investments abroad	+6·2	
Other	+3·4	
Imports of goods and services		−37·9
Merchandise		−25·5
Services		−12·4
Transportation	−2·9	
Travel	−2·7	
Income on foreign investments in the U.S.	−2·1	
Other	−4·7	
Balance on goods and services		+5·1
Unilateral transfers, net		−2·9
Private remittances	−0·6	
U.S. Government Grants and other	−2·3	
Capital Account		−1·8
Transactions in U.S. assets and investments abroad, net		−5·7
Private		−4·2
Direct	−3·5	
Portfolio	−0·3	
Short-term	−0·4	
U.S. Government (excluding official reserve assets)		−1·5

Transactions in foreign assets and investments		
in the U.S., net		*+3·3*
Private		+4·8
Direct	+0·1	
Portfolio	+2·0	
Short-term	+2·7	
Official		−1·5
Long-term	+0·1	
Short-term	−1·6	

Transactions in U.S. official reserve assets, net	*+0·6*

Errors and Omissions, net	*−0·3*

Note: Detail does not add to total because of rounding.

Table 1b
United Kingdom Balance of Payments, 1966, in billions of
dollars (Bank of England)

Current Account		*−0·2*

Exports of goods and services		*+22·0*
Merchandise		+14·4
Services		+7·6
Transportation	+2·7	
Travel	+0·6	
Income on U.K. investments abroad	+2·6	
Other	+1·8	

Imports of goods and services		*−21·5*
Merchandise		−14·8
Services		−6·7
Transportation	−2·5	
Travel	−0·8	
Income on foreign investments in the U.K.	−1·6	
Other	−1·8	

Balance on goods and services	*+0·5*

Unilateral transfers, net	−0·7
Private remittances	−0·2
U.K. Government grants and other	−0·5
Capital Account	+0·2

Transactions in U.K. assets and investments abroad, net		−2·1
Private		−1·5
Direct	−0·9	
Portfolio	−	
Short-term	−0·6	
U.K. Government (excluding official reserve assets)		−0·6

Transactions in foreign assets and investments in the U.K., net		+2·0
Private		+0·5
Direct	+0·6	
Portfolio	+0·1	
Short-term	−0·2	
Official		+1·5
Long-term	+0·2	
Short-term	+1·3	

Transactions in U.K. official reserve assets, net	+0·3
Errors and Omissions, net	—

vices or a regular recipient of grants or reparations. Apart from this qualification, though, in the end we are compelled to admit that there may be some practical sense to this viewpoint, at least within the limited context of balance-of-payments policy. It is, after all, much easier for the financial authorities to maintain over-all payments balance when the balance of trade is in surplus than when it is in deficit.

In 1966, as in most other recent years, the United States clearly had a 'favourable' balance of trade, merchandise exports exceeding imports by more than $3·5 billion. In addition, the United States again earned more than it spent on services – the so-called 'invisible' exports and imports. Americans certainly paid more abroad for transportation and travel than did foreigners in the United States, but on the other hand American foreign investments earned far more income than did foreign investments in the United States. The interest and dividends earned on foreign capital expenditure are generally included among the invisibles of the current account. This income is regarded as a return for services rendered by capital lent abroad.

The United Kingdom had a typically 'unfavourable' balance of trade in 1966. However, in the usual manner this was more than offset by a surplus in the invisibles sector, specifically by a surplus of investment income. Like the United States, the United Kingdom is an international creditor: the British earn far more from their investments abroad than do foreign investors from their assets and investments in Great Britain.

In contrast to the surpluses earned on their sales of goods and services, both the United States and the United Kingdom incurred in 1966, as in most other recent years, substantial deficits on unilateral transfers. As usual, private remittances in both instances were sizeable. However, by far the largest debits here were again attributable to the continuing programme of official grants by each country for foreign economic and military assistance. Why are donations like these recorded in the current account, with exports and imports of goods and services? In at least one important respect transfers differ from current trade: they confer purchasing power on their recipients without a *quid pro quo* in the form of income produced. Nevertheless, on the basis of modern income theory, we may argue that donations belong properly in the current account; they are a unique part of the invisible sector. Certainly private remittances belong there. They come mainly out of the current incomes of the donors, and they enter normally into the consumption of the beneficiaries. Moreover, they tend to be made on a recurring basis which changes slowly from year to year. This is not true of many official donations, such as grants, which are once-for-all transfers of purchasing power more akin to capital investments than to current trade. But precisely because such transfers are in fact final, they are very unlike a capital transaction, which by definition either gives rise to a claim or debt, or takes place in settlement of a claim or debt. A logical case can be made, therefore, for including these, too, in the current account. So defined, the current account shows exactly (with opposite sign) any change in the international investment position of a country. In these illustrations we have adhered to the usual practice of entering all transfers, official as well as private, in the current account.

In the capital account we find all changes in claims on or of the reporting country owned or owed by other countries. These are generally divided into three major categories of transactions. The first comprises all investments by residents abroad, which in 1966, as in most other post-war years, were considerable for both the United States and the United Kingdom. As usual, by far the larger part of the total for each country was accounted for by private investments, particularly by the direct extension of national enterprise overseas. Portfolio investments, mainly long-term bank loans and net purchases of new foreign securities issues, were not large in either instance, and nor were the short-term investments, mainly bank loans and commercial credit. Government investments abroad consist principally of loans to foreign official agencies for economic assistance or military purposes.

The second category of transactions in the capital account consists of all investments in the reporting country by foreign residents, which in 1966 exceeded $3 billion in the case of the United States and approximated to $2 billion in the case of the United Kingdom. Of great interest in both cases here are the foreign official investments listed.

Many of these involve liquid dollar and sterling liabilities,[2] which together with gold make up the major portion of the world's monetary reserves. The dollar and the pound sterling are the world's principal 'reserve' currencies. Governments accumulating reserves and preferring to hold earning assets rather than sterile gold hoards tend to invest in liquid assets denominated either in dollars or – if the country is a member of the so-called sterling area – in sterling. In 1966, however, because interest rates on non-liquid U.S. assets soared, official agencies actually divested themselves of more than $1·5 billion of lower-yielding liquid *dollar* claims. (Many of these were sold to non-official foreigners, thus helping to account for the unusually steep rise of private short-term investments in the United States that year.) Officially owned liquid *sterling* claims, on the other hand, rose once again.

'Transactions in official reserve assets' refer to changes in the monetary gold stock of the financial authorities, in official holdings of convertible foreign currencies, and in the country's net position in the International Monetary Fund (I.M.F.). Movements here in 1966 were small for both the United States and the United Kingdom.

Since the balance of payments is constructed as an accounting identity, with each transaction theoretically recorded twice, the sum total of debits and credits should in theory always be equal. That is, the current account and the capital account should always be equal (with signs reversed). But in fact this is rarely the case. In practice it is difficult to collect data on both sides of every transaction. Usually, the various entries – exports and imports, transfers, capital and reserve transactions – can only be tabulated or estimated singly, by methods of varying degrees of accuracy, and then summed. As a result, despite the best efforts of statisticians, the current and capital accounts rarely 'balance' statistically. In 1966, there happened to be no significant discrepancy in the balance of payments of

2. By liquid liabilities is generally meant all short-term liabilities to foreigners other than commercial credits and brokers' balances.

the United Kingdom. There was, however, a discrepancy of some $300 million in the balance of payments of the United States, even though the American data are among the most accurate in the world. In some instances, the coverage of the data tends to be inadequate; it is known that for several reasons some important items still manage to escape the statisticians' net. In other instances, errors are committed in the process of estimation; such inaccuracies are virtually impossible to avoid. Problems also arise in trying to consolidate without duplication the data collected from independent sources by a variety of techniques. To the extent that these empirical deficiencies cause the observed totals of debits and credits to differ, it is necessary to add a balancing item for 'errors and omissions'. Every payments account has one. Its purpose is to ensure that in accordance with the theory of double-entry book-keeping, the balance of payments always balances in an accounting sense.

Relationship to other social accounts

What is the significance of the fact that, apart from 'errors and omissions', the current account must always equal the capital account (with signs reversed)? It means that if increases in claims on foreigners are to exceed increases in liabilities to foreigners by any amount – that is, if a country is to be able to invest abroad – exports must be made to exceed imports.[3] There must be a credit on current account to match the debit on capital account. Conversely, a country may borrow abroad only to the extent that it can promote a net inward movement of real goods and services. For a net financial transfer to occur, a real transfer must occur.

This does not mean that each individual transfer of

3. Here and in the remainder of this volume, except where otherwise indicated, imports are interpreted to include unilateral transfers abroad, since like purchases of goods and services, these confer purchasing power on foreigners. By the same token, exports are understood to include unilateral transfers received.

financial assets must be accompanied by a corresponding transfer of real goods or services. We are speaking of *net* flows here. For the most part, individual transactions in financial claims just do not operate that way. Persons or corporations generally invest or borrow abroad simply by exchanging certain types of assets or liabilities for other types of assets or liabilities. Mr Jones, for example, an imaginary Cohenian investor, buys a foreign bond, paying with dollars. For Mr Jones, this transaction, which is listed as a debit in the balance of payments of Cohenia (with the increase of dollar liabilities recorded as a credit), constitutes a capital outflow: he is deliberately sending his money abroad for investment purposes. For the country as a whole, though, this is not yet a capital outflow; it is simply an exchange of short-term liabilities for a long-term asset. For the country as a whole, an export of capital can be accomplished only on a net basis, by a corresponding transfer of real goods or services.

In fact, to be precise about the matter, the transfer of goods or services itself *is* the capital export; it is what economists call a 'real transfer'. The corresponding movement of financial assets, while obviously related to the real transfer,[4] is not itself a true capital movement. It is merely a 'monetary transfer', a movement of financial capital. For the movement of financial capital to translate itself into a true foreign loan or investment, a real movement of capital must take place: the country must somehow export goods and services above the value of the goods it imports. Otherwise, what Mr Jones naïvely thinks is a foreign investment will be for the country collectively not a net increase of foreign financial claims but rather merely an exchange of one type of asset for another. By the same token, a country cannot borrow from abroad, in a real sense, except to the extent that its current account is in deficit. The excess of

4. In our example, the movement of financial assets gives rise to the real transfer. The relationship could of course be the other way around: the real transfer could give rise to the movement of financial assets. The net financial transfer may be cause or effect.

imports over exports is the real transfer of capital; the corresponding net increase of foreign liabilities is itself merely a monetary transfer.

This point can be summarized in notation form:
Current account = capital account;

$$X - M = I_\text{f},$$

where X represents exports of goods and services, M imports, and I_f net foreign investment. When the current account is in surplus, exports exceeding imports, the country is investing abroad; when it is in deficit, the country is borrowing (disinvesting) abroad.

These propositions simply restate the elementary economic identity that any difference between the current receipts of an individual economic unit and its current expenditures must equal the change in its net investment position. When income exceeds spending in the current period, the unit is investing (saving); when spending exceeds income, it is disinvesting (using savings or borrowing). Thus it is not only in accordance with the theory of double-entry book-keeping that the balance of payments must always balance. It is also in accordance with the fundamental theory of economic activity. That the sum of the current and capital accounts of a country must be zero is an economic truism. There can be no net international financial transfer without a corresponding real transfer.

How in practice a country accomplishes the translation of a movement of financial capital into a movement of real capital is essentially explained by the theory of exchange rates, and hence is a subject more appropriately treated in another of the volumes of this series. The matter is raised here for one reason – because it provides the key to understanding the economic relationship between the accounting balance of payments and two other important social accounts. These are the national income and product account and the balance of international indebtedness.

The *national income and product account* is a systematic

statement of the total value of goods and services produced and consumed by the residents of a country during a specified period of time (usually a year). It provides a framework within which the current operations of the economy can be recorded. Like the balance-of-payments account, the national income and product account is constructed according to the principles of double-entry book-keeping. On the debit side are listed the 'allocations' of national income: consumption, saving and taxes. On the credit side are listed the 'sources' of national income, categorized in terms of the alternative modes of expenditure on domestic product. In a theoretical closed economy, where there are neither exports nor imports, the only sources of national income are domestic private expenditures on consumption and investment and government spending. But in the real world all economies are open, buying and selling abroad in varying degrees. Hence it is necessary to add foreign expenditure on exports as an additional source of national income, and to deduct domestic expenditures on imports (which are a use of national income). Of course, as an accounting identity the national income and product account must always 'balance': the allocations of national income must just equal the sources of national income.

Tables 2a and 2b present consolidated statements of the 1966 national income and product of, respectively the United States and the United Kingdom. It should be noted that the figures for exports correspond to those listed in Tables 1a and 1b; the figures for imports include both purchases of foreign goods and services and net unilateral transfers abroad. Despite the relatively large size of these transfers, foreign transactions on balance added to the national income of both countries in 1966 (though not by much in relative terms).

Like the balance-of-payments account, the national income and product account can be summarized in notation form:

$$C + S + T = C + I + G + (X - M),$$

where C represents consumer expenditures, S domestic saving, T tax payments, I investment expenditures, and G government spending. It is manifest that in a closed economy the total of domestic expenditures $(C+I+G)$ can neither exceed nor fall short of current income $(C+S+T)$: *ex post*, net domestic intake – what most economists today call 'real absorption' – must just equal national income. In notation form:

$$Y = A,$$

where $Y = C+S+T =$ real income,

and $A = C+I+G =$ real absorption.

Furthermore, if the government budget is balanced (or if the net budget deficit or surplus is consolidated as part of net domestic saving), this implies that in a closed economy, *ex post*, domestic investment cannot differ from the volume of domestic saving:

$$S_\mathrm{d} = I_\mathrm{d}.$$

only to the extent that exports are less than or greater than imports – that is, only to the extent that there is a net deficit However, these equalities are not a requirement of an open economy. With foreign trade included, domestic absorption can exceed or fall short of national income, but or surplus in the current account of the balance of payments. Conversely, there can be no net current-account surplus or deficit except to the extent that the domestic economy absorbs less or more than its current income:

$$Y \gtrless A = X \gtrless M.$$

Alternatively, $S_\mathrm{d} \gtrless I_\mathrm{d} = X \gtrless M = \pm I_\mathrm{f}$ (net foreign investment).

What this means is that a country cannot lend or invest abroad, via a current-account surplus, unless it is able to 'save' the current domestic output needed to accomplish the real transfer. The volume of domestic investment must be suppressed below the level of domestic saving. By the same token, a country cannot invest for domestic purposes

Table 2a
United States National Income and Product, 1966, in billions of dollars (U.S. Department of Commerce, Office of Business Economics)

Allocations		Sources		
Consumption	466·5	Consumers' expenditures		466·5
Savings	56·8	Investment	,,	54·5
Taxes	156·5	Government	,,	156·6
		Exports		43·0
		Minus: imports		−40·8
	679·8			679·8

Table 2b
United Kingdom National Income and Product, 1966, in billions of dollars (U.K. Central Statistical Office)

Allocations		Sources		
Consumption	67·5	Consumers' expenditures		67·5
Savings	19·4	Investment	,,	19·2
Taxes	18·2	Government	,,	17·9
		Exports		22·0
		Minus: imports		−21·5
	105·1			105·1

beyond the level of its own savings except to the extent that it is able to borrow or attract investments from abroad. We shall return to this point shortly.

The *balance of international indebtedness* is a systematic statement of the total claims of a country's residents on foreign countries and of the total claims of residents of foreign countries on its residents. Since the balance of indebtedness is a record of a stock rather than of a flow, it differs from both the balance-of-payments account and the national income and product account in one important respect: rather than covering a specified period of time, as do the others, it is related to a given point of time, such as the end of the year. Still, like the others, the balance of indebtedness is constructed according to the principles of double-entry book-keeping. A country's international assets and liabilities are summed, and the difference between them is labelled 'net worth'. When net worth is positive, a country is a creditor in international financial affairs. Otherwise it is a debtor.

Tables 3a and 3b present consolidated statements of the balance of indebtedness of, respectively, the United States and the United Kingdom at the end of 1966. It will be noted that both countries are international creditors, America very substantially so with foreign assets nearly double liabilities. Most of the two countries' assets, however, including those of both governments, are of long-term rather than short-term maturity, whereas the opposite is true of each country's liabilities. In the United States this fact concerning the debt structure of the national investment position has taken on a crucial importance in the debate over balance-of-payments policy, as we shall see in chapter 4.

It is clear from the nature of these accounts that apart from variations in the current market value of outstanding claims and liabilities, no change is possible in a country's balance of international indebtedness, except to the extent that there is a net inward or outward movement of financial claims – that is, to the extent that there is a net deficit or surplus in the capital account of the balance of payments ($\pm I_f$). But we have already emphasized that for a financial transfer to occur – say, an outward movement of funds ($+I_f$) – a real transfer must take place ($X > M$). And from our discussion of the national income and product account we know that for a real transfer to take place, the country must be prepared to absorb less than its current output ($Y > A$). In short, a net improvement of a country's international investment position requires that it reduce national absorption relative to national income. It must

Table 3a
United States Balance of International Indebtedness, 1966, in billions of dollars (U.S. Department of Commerce, Office of Business Economics)

U.S. assets and investments abroad, total		*111·9*
Government		25·6
Private		86·3
Long-term	75·6	
Short-term	10·7	
Foreign assets and investments in the U.S., total		*60·4*
Long-term		27·0
Short-term		33·4

Table 3b
United Kingdom Balance of International Indebtedness, 1966, in billions of dollars (Bank of England)

U.K. assets and investments abroad, total		*49·8*
Government		8·8
Private		41·0
Long-term	26·9	
Short-term	14·1	
Foreign assets and investments in the U.K., total		*45·9*
Long-term		18·9
Short-term		27·0

'save' a portion of its resources so that they can be invested abroad. Conversely, if a country is willing to see its international creditor–debtor position deteriorate, it can 'dissave', borrowing abroad in order to 'live beyond its means'. In notation form:

$$\pm I_f = Y \gtrless A.$$

Measurement of 'balance'

The fact that the balance of payments always balances in an accounting sense does not mean that a country never experiences payments difficulties. Quite the opposite. Over-all payments balance requires equality not of the sum total of debits and credits but of certain categories of debits and credits. Surpluses and deficits are defined in terms of certain groupings of items which are segregated from the main body of the balance of payments as being different in some significant respect from the rest. The question is this: which items? What is the proper measure of 'balance'?

The balance of international indebtedness reflects net inward or outward movements of capital, as recorded in the capital account of the balance of payments. Does this mean that the total capital account is the proper measure of balance? Not at all. The balance of indebtedness is a 'stock' account, analogous to (though not identical with) the balance sheet of a corporate enterprise. It is designed to show the international investment position of the reporting country at a single point of time. Its main concern is with considerations of solvency – with increases and decreases of national 'net worth' – and it is in this connexion that the total capital balance is particularly useful. But the payments account itself is a 'flow' concept, analogous to (though not identical with) the income statement of a corporate enterprise rather than to the balance sheet. It is designed to show what happens to the current international economic relationships of the reporting country over a period of time. As such, its main concern is not with considerations of solvency but of liquidity – with increases or decreases of foreign liquid assets (including official reserves) and liabilities. These are money assets and liabilities having a sufficient degree of liquidity to be regarded as means of international payment. The measure of surplus or deficit in the balance of payments should reflect changes in the net liquidity position of the country. This total capital balance cannot do.

To identify changes in the net liquidity position of a country, we must look to certain items within the total capital account. To begin with, it is convenient to distinguish between two types of transactions in the balance of payments. These are autonomous transactions and accommodating (induced, compensatory) transactions (Meade, 1951, ch. 1).

Autonomous transactions are undertaken for their own sake – for the profit they entail or the satisfaction they yield. They have their source in the fundamental differences between countries in prices, incomes, and interest rates, and they take place regardless of the size of the other items in the balance of payments. They are voluntary and deliberate in character. Autonomous transactions comprise virtually all exports and imports of goods and services, since these are generally undertaken directly for the profit to be made. They also include unilateral transfers, which are generally intended to reduce deliberately fundamental differences between the incomes of individuals or of nations. And finally, they include most long-term capital movements as well as the many short-term capital movements motivated by a desire either to earn a higher return, to make a speculative gain, or to find a safe refuge for one's capital.

Accommodating transactions, by contrast, are not undertaken for their own sake at all. Rather, they have their source in the other (autonomous) transactions elsewhere in the balance of payments. They take place, not regardless of the size of the other items in the account, but precisely because the other items are such as to leave a gap to be filled. They accommodate such gaps, sometimes automatically (as when foreign-exchange dealers adjust for increases or decreases of their working balances, or when governments intervene in the foreign-exchange market to support their exchange rates) and sometimes by choice (such as when special aid is provided by the banking system or the government of a surplus country). Accommodating transactions consist almost entirely of cash payments or receipts (including transactions in official reserves).[5] They are the *residual* money flows in the balance of payments – and as such they reflect increases or decreases of the liquidity of a country. They are, therefore, the best measure of surplus or deficit in the balance of payments.

Thus we conclude that a deficit appears in the balance of payments when autonomous transactions requiring money payments exceed autonomous transactions involving money receipts. The deficit means that the country is losing liquidity to others: it is running down its liquid foreign assets (including offical reserve assets) and/or accumulating liquid foreign liabilities. Conversely, a surplus exists when autonomous money receipts exceed autonomous payments.

It follows that surpluses and deficits could be identified rather easily if we could simply place all autonomous transactions inside the main body of the balance of payments ('above the line') and all accommodating transactions outside it ('below the line'). But in fact the process of measuring 'balance' – of drawing the 'line' – is not nearly so elementary. For while the analytical distinction between autonomous transactions and accommodating transactions is useful in theory (and in the formulation of balance-of-payments policy, as we shall see), it is of hardly any use in practice. The empirical difficulties associated with it are enormous. Specifically, it is impossible to identify, from the bare statistical data, the motivations of individual transactions – that is, to determine which transactions are undertaken for their own sake and which have their source in other transactions elsewhere in the account. Consequently, it is impossible, empirically, to distinguish autonomous and accommodating transactions at all, except to the extent that it is possible to associate the motivations of transactions

5. There are exceptions, of course, such as the movements of goods which correspond to a 'unilateral transfer in kind' or foreign investments involving the shipment abroad of domestic plant and equipment. These are accommodating transactions, too. But in relative terms these exceptions do not in fact figure prominently in the balance of payments. For the purposes of our discussion they can be ignored.

with certain classes of transactions or with certain types of transactions which are observable. The definition of surplus or deficit is an analytical problem, but the accounting framework of measurement is essentially classificatory – and there are limitless way of arranging the data to make it as informative as possible for particular questions. There is therefore no unique, 'right', measure of balance, only alternative observed measures which, given the country and the time period, more or less closely approximate to the precise analytical concept.

Since the number of alternative measures is in fact so large, any one country would be well advised to employ a variety of them in order to derive the most complete picture of its international payments position. Most countries, though, seem to prefer a simple, clear, straightforward, if possibly misleading, definition – a single summary measure of surplus or deficit. It is possible to classify the existing national concepts into two broad categories which shade into one another. These are the 'basic' balance and the 'official-settlements' balance.

The *basic balance* places only current-account transactions and long-term capital movements 'above the line'. These are supposed to make up the autonomous transactions that determine the 'basic' course of the balance of payments. 'Below the line' are placed all short-term capital flows and the errors and omissions item (changes in which are believed to reflect mainly unrecorded movements of private short-term capital) as well as official reserve transactions. The reason given for including short-term capital flows below the line is that all such transactions may be considered accommodating, some responding passively to the balance on other transactions, others to short-term changes in monetary policy and credit conditions. A second rationale for this division is that it segregates below the line the transactions most prone to volatile and possibly erratic shifts. The basic transactions above the line, by contrast, are presumed to be fairly stable in the short run, and in the long run to change only gradually in response to the broad forces at work in the domestic and international economy.

As an attempt to identify underlying trends in the balance of payments, the basic-balance concept is a rather useful one, and it forms in fact the basis for several national measures of balance. But as an attempt to approximate closely to the analytical distinction between autonomous and accommodating transactions the concept is defective, for the dichotomy underlying it is quite artificial. The basic balance distinguishes between types of transactions, specifically between long-term and short-term capital. In actual fact, though, these types of transactions are in many ways not so dissimilar. There are as often persistent trends in short-term capital movements as in the so-called basic transactions, just as there are as often large transitory elements in the latter as in the former. Not all short-term capital flows are responsive to monetary policy, however; many are not, and indeed many are not accommodating in any sense at all. In the same way, certain so-called basic items, particularly in the portfolio-investment and merchandise-trade accounts, do appear to be responsive to monetary policy. Private financial transactions just cannot be divided satisfactorily along this dimension. As Richard Cooper has observed:

... unfortunately the sensitivity of various international transactions to monetary policy varies along a continuum, so any dichotomy into 'policy-sensitive' and 'not policy-sensitive' is necessarily artificial; and over time both the sensitivity of transactions to policy and the policy instruments themselves are likely to change, so the aptness of any particular dichotomy will probably be short-lived (Cooper, 1966, p. 385).

For these reasons, an alternative to the basic-balance concept is used by a number of countries – and urged for all countries by the International Monetary Fund. This is the *official-settlements balance,* which distinguishes not between types of transactions but rather between types of transactors. All private short-term capital movements are placed above the line, as also is the errors and omissions item. Only official reserve transactions are included below the line, on the grounds that these alone, reflecting official intervention in the foreign-exchange market, truly represent accommodating flows. The reason given is that these are the transactions of the only transactors whose *function* it is to be accommodating under the present international monetary system. Only the financial authorities have the responsibility for maintaining stable exchange rates. Their gains and losses of reserve assets and liabilities to foreign official authorities provide the best index of the financing required by surpluses and deficits, and hence constitute the most accurate measure of balance.

However, objections can be raised to this concept, too – objections which are essentially the converse of those raised to the basic-balance concept. It is a fact, for instance, that at least some private short-term capital flows – bank loans to finance trade, commercial credits and the like – are truly accommodating in the full sense of the term. At the same time, certain official transactions have nothing at all to do with financing gaps in the balance of payments in the current period. Occasionally, central banks decide to borrow in foreign capital markets to augment their reserves, or to sell reserves to domestic commercial banks when they want to drain internal liquidity. These decisions are no less autonomous than the decisions by private transactors to trade or invest abroad.

The basic-balance and official-settlements concepts are illustrated schematically in Table 4. The table follows the same general format as Tables 1a and 1b, itemizing all of the major categories of transactions usually distinguished in the balance of payments. Alternative measures of surplus or deficit are defined by the different 'lines' that are drawn segregating transactions 'above' from transactions 'below'. An extreme formulation of the official-settlements concept, shown at the bottom of the list, includes below the line only changes in gross monetary reserves, excluding changes in the country's foreign liquid liabilities. However, this procedure is not common. Usually, liquid liabilities to foreign official institutions are also included, as in the more conventional version of the official-settlements balance shown second from the bottom. Additionally, other items can be included in the financing of surplus or deficit, such as (a) changes in liquid liabilities to private foreigners, (b) changes in liquid foreign assets privately held by residents, and (c) the errors and omissions item. As more of these are shifted below the line, the concept of basic balance is approached more and more closely. When all of them are shifted down, as the table shows, basic balance is identified.

Most countries employ some 'hybrid' of the two main concepts as their national measure of balance. Two such national measures are listed in Table 4 – those of the United Kingdom and the United States. The British measure of balance closely approximates to the basic-balance concept, the only significant difference being that errors and omissions are placed above rather than below the line. The British authorities believe that the so-called 'balancing item' mainly reflects gaps in their trade and long-term investment statistics rather than movements of unrecorded short-term capital. Therefore, they segregate the item from the remainder of private short-term capital and official reserve transactions, which are collectively labelled 'monetary movements' in the standard U. K. account. These monetary movements define surplus or deficit in the British balance of payments (Bank of England, 1964).

To define surplus or deficit in the American balance of payments, the United States adopted in 1955 a measure which has been named the 'over-all' or 'liquidity' balance. This measure places below the line all official reserve transactions, including changes in both gross reserves and in liquid liabilities to foreign official institutions; in addition, it includes changes in liquid liabilities to private foreigners as well. Changes in liquid foreign assets privately held by Americans, however, are placed above the line. Thus the concept is asymmetrical. It combines two separate distinctions: for U.S. assets abroad, the distinction is (as in the official-transactions concept) by type of transactor, official

Table 4
Alternative Measures of Payments Balance, Surplus or Deficit

Categories of Transactions	*Alternative Measures of Balance*
Exports of goods and services Imports of goods and services Unilateral transfers, net Transactions in long-term capital, net	
	Basic balance
Errors and omissions, net ('balancing item')	
	United Kingdom ('monetary movements')
Private transactions in short-term assets and investments abroad (changes in liquid foreign assets privately held by residents), net	
	United States ('over-all', 'liquidity')
Private transactions in short-term assets and investments in country of residence (changes in liquid liabilities to private foreigners), net	
	Official settlements (conventional formulation)
Official transactions in short-term assets and investments in country of residence (changes in liquid liabilities to foreign official institutions), net	
	Official settlements (extreme formulation)
Transactions in official reserve assets, net	

versus others; for foreign assets in the United States, the distinction is (as in the basic-balance concept) by type of transaction, short-term versus long-term.

The liquidity or over-all balance concept originated in the Balance-of-Payments Division of the United States Department of Commerce, and from its inception was staunchly defended by the Division's chief, Walther Lederer, the official responsible for compiling the U.S. payments statistics (Lederer, 1963). Essentially, Lederer argued that since it is so difficult to identify the motivations of individual transactions – that is, to know which are autonomous and which are accommodating – it is not worth trying. Instead, the balance of payments should attempt to measure directly changes in the ability of the government to defend the exchange value of its currency. This, according to Lederer, is the proper measure of the net liquidity position of a country. In general, the capability of a government to defend its exchange rate depends upon the liquid resources available to the financial authorities for use in the foreign-exchange market, and upon the liquid claims that can be exercised against these resources. In the specific instance of the United States, Lederer argued, the only liquid resources available to the financial authorities are their own monetary reserves. The foreign assets of the private American economy cannot be included because no direct controls exist by which they might be effectively mobilized for this purpose. On the other hand, though, liabilities to private foreigners as well as those to foreign official institutions have to be counted among the liquid claims that can be exercised against these resources, because foreign private holdings in many countries are closely controlled by central banks and hence are not very different from official holdings in their significance for the United States. Besides, foreign private holdings of dollars are heavily concentrated in very liquid claims, such as deposits and short-term Treasury securities, whereas private U.S. holdings of foreign claims are rather less liquid, being mainly bank loans and acceptances and commercial credits.

Lederer's arguments could be criticized on a number of grounds. In the first place his definition of the liquidity position of a country was manifestly a rather special one, hardly corresponding to the concept of net money flows which most economists contend is the proper basis for measuring balance. Furthermore, even in terms of his own definition, which stresses the ability of a government to defend its exchange rate, Lederer's arguments seemed on the one hand to draw too sharp and artificial a distinction between private foreigners and private U.S. residents, while on the other hand they failed to distinguish adequately between private foreigners and foreign financial authorities. The liquidity-balance concept implies that U.S. reserve assets are needed to protect the dollar only against withdrawals of foreign holdings, whereas historical experience demonstrates that outflows of domestic capital typically play a leading role in payments deficits and speculative runs on a currency. At the same time, it implies that all foreign holdings represent an equal threat to the dollar, whereas in fact only foreign financial authorities can directly draw down U.S. reserves. In a real sense, therefore, as well as in an accounting sense, the concept is asymmetrical: depending on the perspective, it includes either too little or too much to be useful as a direct measure of the ability of the United States Government to defend the dollar.

For these reasons, in the late 1950s and early 1960s, a number of American economists, most notably Hal Lary of the National Bureau of Economic Research, advocated replacing the liquidity measure with one of the variants of the basic-balance concept (Lary, 1963). Alternatively, some observers, including for instance Peter Kenen, advocated changing over to the official-settlements concept (Kenen, 1964). In 1963 a committee of prominent economists, chaired by Edward M. Bernstein, was appointed by the U.S. Bureau of the Budget to review the issue, and in 1965 issued a Report favouring the latter course (Balance of Payments Statistics Review Committee, 1965, ch. 9). The report stressed, however, that 'No single number can adequately describe the international position of the United States during any given period.... We explicitly reject ... the notion that as a practical matter people must view the balance of payments position in terms of a single summary concept, the surplus or deficit' (Balance of Payments Statistics Review Committee, 1965, p. 101). And indeed, when the official settlements concept was adopted officially by the Commerce Department in 1966, it was as a complement to, not as a substitute for, the traditional liquidity concept. Today both measures are used to identify surplus or deficit in the United States balance of payments.

Implications for policy

The United States is now an exception in this respect. Nearly all other countries continue to apply a single summary concept of deficit or surplus to their balance of payments, despite the common knowledge that there is no one 'right' measure of balance. This practice has important implications for the formation and conduct of balance-of-payments policy.

In the first place, it implies that for any one country, defects of measurement will frequently be transformed into defects of policy (Cooper, 1966, pp. 390–4). Generally, the financial authorities aim to maintain a 'balance' of autonomous money payments and receipts.[6] In the accounting balance of payments, however, all they have to work with is some one observed measure of balance more or less closely approximating to the precise analytical concept. A problem for policy arises when officials set empirical balance as their target variable, having in mind autonomous balance. To the extent that the two targets differ because of errors in the conception or measurement of the former, public

6. Of course, there may be times when 'balance' of autonomous money payments and receipts is not considered to be the proper aim of the financial authorities – when it is thought that prolonged payments surpluses or deficits would better serve important economic objectives – but that is a matter which goes beyond the issues of concern here. However, see below, chapters 3 and 4.

policy will be misguided. The authorities will be operating on the basis of an incorrect perception of the size of the correction needed to restore and maintain a balance of autonomous transactions.

Moreover, the danger of defective policy is compounded by a further danger of conflict among national policies, owing to the fact that different countries use different measures of balance (Høst-Madsen, 1962). Analytically, all deficits and surpluses have their counterparts; taken together, they should add to zero. But as far as the accounting balance of payments is concerned, no such symmetry between total surpluses and total deficits exists, because of the asymmetry of national concepts.[7] Most countries, it has been noted, use some hybrid of the two main concepts of balance. Like the traditional liquidity measure employed by the United States, many other national concepts commonly in use distinguish roughly between changes in the foreign-exchange holdings of residents, which are placed above the line inside the main body of the account, and the corresponding liabilities to foreigners, which are included below the line. Accordingly, an increase of private foreign-exchange holdings, such as has taken place in recent years, tends to create an excess of total deficits over total surpluses. The excess is not small, and it is magnified by other, additional discrepancies that have been perceived in national concepts and definitions (Smith, 1967). The excess is significant to the extent that individual governments set empirical balance as their target variable. Since balance-of-payments targets set by all countries taken together will themselves add at least to zero (and perhaps to an excess of surpluses over deficits), the actual excess of total deficits

7. Actually, even if all national concepts were identical, there would still be one significant source of asymmetry between total deficits and total surpluses: the increase in world gold holdings. In general, the sales of gold-producing countries are treated as commodity exports, but changes in official gold reserves are always included below the line. *Ceteris paribus*, total surpluses will exceed total deficits by the magnitude of the increase in world monetary gold holdings (Høst-Madsen, 1962, p. 187).

implies considerable conflict among such targets – and therefore considerable conflict among national policies as well.

The principal implication of all this is that the accounting balance by itself is an insufficient information base for formulating and conducting payments policy. To use it alone in setting official target variables is to misapply it. Rather, it is best applied as a supplement to other tools of analysis. Certainly the account does have its uses. It can provide the authorities with a complete statistical record of a country's international economic relations. Moreover, if successive years are compared, the authorities can identify in concise fashion changes in the country's commercial and financial status, and hence pinpoint areas of strength and weakness. In short, the accounting balance can be a rather powerful instrument for *ex post description* of events. But it is *not* a very strong instrument for *ex ante analysis* of events. Being essentially a classificatory device, the accounting balance can do little more than indicate, in an approximate fashion, the extent of balance or imbalance of *past* transactions. The authorities need to know this. But even more importantly, they need to know, and in as precise a fashion as possible, the extent of balance or imbalance of *present* and *future* transactions – that is, the extent of 'equilibrium' or 'disequilibrium' of autonomous, *intended* transactions. What is happening currently to the net liquidity position of the country? Are autonomous money payments in the near future likely to exceed or fall short of anticipated money receipts? For the authorities the main problem is analytical, not descriptive. For this purpose, the accounting balance is inconvenient and cumbersome. Of more interest are the remaining two concepts of balance, which will now be discussed.

The Programme Balance

The programme balance of payments of a country is a systematic statement of sources and uses of foreign funds, expected or planned, over a future period of one or more years. It is based upon a calculation of domestic consumption and investment requirements, and upon a programme of meeting an excess of requirements over resources by recourse to foreign finance expected or sought. Essentially it is a forecast of the country's foreign-exchange (foreign-currency) needs and desires – a kind of accounting balance of the future, so to speak. Deficits and surpluses are defined in terms of the gaps between these needs and desires on the one hand, and on the other hand the amounts of foreign exchange expected to become available from all regular sources (exports, foreign investments, etc.).

Not all countries compute a complete programme balance of payments. The concept originated as a supplement to mechanisms developed for national planning of the domestic economy. It is most useful to countries regularly dependent on foreign financial assistance to sustain certain levels of home consumption and capital formation. It indicates the amount of financing that will be needed and for how long. Today, its use is confined almost entirely to the countries of the less developed areas of the world.

The *ex ante* character of the programme balance is self-evident. Being a prognosis of future developments, it provides the financial authorities with a useful tool for analysing the appropriateness of current policies and plans affecting the country's international economic position. But it must be stressed that the prognosis is a highly subjective one. Foreign financing requirements are projected in relation to certain accepted standards of needs and desires, that is, in relation to certain levels of domestic consumption and certain rates of domestic investment which, in this context, are matters of political judgement. If financing potentialities change, so too are these standards likely to be altered. The programme balance is as much based on psychology as it is on economics. By itself, therefore, the programme balance is no more useful for the purpose of formulating and conducting payments policy than is the accounting balance. Like the latter, it is best applied as a supplement to other tools of analysis – in particular, the market balance of payments.

The Market Balance

The market balance of payments of a country can best be understood as a model of a given situation in the foreign-exchange market, characterized by the effective demand and supply of foreign exchange at the current exchange rate and at alternative, hypothetical rates. It is an *ex ante* concept, comparing autonomous spending and receipts given present and expected future incomes, prices, and interest rates. Demand and supply are conceived in terms of schedules. The demand for foreign exchange represents the sum of the demands of importers, donors abroad, investors and the like, all of whom must usually purchase foreign currencies in order to consummate their intended external transactions. Correspondingly, since foreign transactors must generally sell their own currencies for local currency in order to effect local payments, the supply of foreign exchange represents the sum of foreign donations and foreign demands for the country's exports, securities, etc. Like any other price, the price of foreign exchange – the rate of exchange – is the product of the interaction of the demand and supply schedules.

The market balance of payments describes currently, as the accounting balance of payments describes historically, the balance of autonomous international transactions. However, it should be noted that the coverage of the market balance does not quite match up to that of the accounting balance. In the latter we find not only virtually all foreign-exchange transactions[8] but also many entries which, since they represent essentially book-keeping operations, never pass through the exchange market at all. These include,

8. The only significant exceptions are the occasional direct sales of foreign exchange by one private firm to another without the intermediation of a bank or foreign-exchange broker. See chapter 2.

most importantly, unilateral transfers in kind, barter deals, and direct investments of plant and equipment. By the same token, we find some transactions which take place entirely in foreign currency and never involve the local currency – such as reinvestments of income earned from foreign subsidiaries or securities. And conversely, we find some transactions which, while technically defined as international economic intercourse, really take place entirely in local currency between residents of the reporting country and never involve any foreign currency. All freight on imports, for instance, may be recorded in the payments account, even that paid to domestically operated carriers. It is manifest, therefore, that the market balance of payments is less comprehensive than the accounting balance of payments. As has been emphasized, the latter provides a more complete picture of the character and dimensions of the country's participation in the world economy.

However, as has also been emphasized, this is not the primary information that the financial authorities need for the purpose of formulating and conducting payments policy. Of the greatest importance is the extent of balance or imbalance of the country's autonomous, *intended* transactions. For this purpose the market balance provides a much more useful tool of analysis than does the accounting balance. The market balance gives an accurate index of current international payments 'equilibrium' or 'disequilibrium'. When the demand for foreign exchange is just equal to the supply at the given exchange rate, the implication is that autonomous transactions requiring foreign money payments must just be equal to autonomous transactions involving money receipts. The balance of payments is currently in 'equilibrium'. When demand and supply are not equal the implication is that autonomous payments and receipts must be out of line. The balance is currently in 'disequilibrium'. The problem of payments adjustment, roughly speaking, is to reconcile any such differences between autonomous demand and supply of foreign exchange at a given exchange rate.[9]

This is the basic issue of payments policy. Indeed, this is what the balance of payments is all about. The essential problem is not to examine the accounting balance, to identify a surplus or deficit in the recent past and match it by an equivalent flow of reserves. For the financial authorities, who are concerned first and foremost with current developments, the accounting balance is practically 'ancient history'; and besides, as we previously noted, it is difficult to know which particular empirical measure *ex post* most closely approximates to autonomous balance *ex ante*. Nor is the essential problem to examine the programme balance, to identify foreign financing requirements in the near future and undertake to bring them in line with foreign financing potentialities. The programme balance is simply too contingent and subjective to be of much use currently. Both of these balances have their uses, as has been emphasized – indeed, this cannot be emphasized enough – and both of these problems often occupy the makers of policy. But they are secondary problems. As far as the financial authorities are concerned, the really basic issue is the market balance. Their main problem is to examine the market balance, to identify pressures on the exchange rate and intervene to eliminate them directly or indirectly. The main problem of balance-of-payments policy, in short, is to manage the foreign-exchange market.

9. These are tentative definitions of 'equilibrium', 'disequilibrium' and 'adjustment'. In chapter 3 we shall examine these notions more closely.

2 The Foreign-Exchange Market

The principal distinguishing characteristic of international economic transactions is that they involve the use of different moneys. Every country issues its own currency: within the national frontiers no currency but the local currency is generally acceptable as the medium of exchange or unit of account. Consequently, producers selling goods abroad must convert foreign money received into domestic money. Likewise, investors holding domestic money must acquire foreign moneys in order to acquire stocks and bonds elsewhere. The medium through which the different national moneys are bought and sold is the foreign-exchange market. The basic function of the market is to transfer purchasing power between countries – that is, to facilitate the interchange between local currency and foreign currencies ('foreign exchange').

The foreign-exchange market is not an organized exchange like the stock or commodity exchanges. It has no centralized meeting place, nor is it limited to any one country. It is best thought of as a mechanism whereby buyers and sellers of foreign exchange are brought together. Essentially it consists of a number of banks actively engaged in the trading of currencies. The banks 'make' the foreign-exchange market: each one maintains an inventory of foreign currencies to which it adds or subtracts in the course of doing business with its regular customers. Clearings are effected through foreign-exchange brokers, who function as middlemen for the banks. The banks, in turn, function as currency wholesalers for foreign traders and investors in general, who are the ultimate participants in the foreign-exchange market. The role of the private participants in the market will be examined in the first section of this chapter. The second section will, in turn, examine the role of the financial authorities in the context of their over-all balance-of-payments policy.

The Private Participants

Foreign exchange is not a homogeneous commodity. The term describes several different forms of short-term monetary claims on foreigners denominated in foreign currency. The quickest means of international payment is provided by the cable (telegraphic) transfer. A cablegram to a foreign bank transfers the ownership of a foreign deposit, denominated in a foreign currency, to the purchaser of that currency. Although a comparatively recent innovation, the cable transfer is, because of the speed and ease with which it can be effected, the most important instrument of foreign exchange today, eclipsing the more traditional instruments – the mail transfer, the bank draft, and various types of foreign bills of exchange.

Spot and forward markets

Foreign exchange bought and sold for immediate delivery[1] is called *spot exchange*. The *spot rate* is simply the price of foreign exchange for such transaction. Since two currencies are involved, the price can be expressed in terms of either monetary unit. There is no standard method of calculating foreign-exchange rates. The usual practice in most countries is to quote foreign currencies in terms of the number of units of local currency required to make one foreign unit. Thus in the United States the rate for, say, the German mark (Deutsche mark) will be quoted as one mark equal to twenty-five cents, whereas in Germany it will be said that four marks cost one dollar. But there are exceptions to this practice, the most important being in the United Kingdom, where foreign-exchange rates are usually

1. Immediate delivery means within one or two business days.

quoted in terms of the number of foreign units required to make one pound sterling.

Foreign exchange is bought and sold not only for immediate delivery but also for future delivery, typically for thirty, sixty, ninety, or one hundred and eighty days, though both longer and shorter contracts are often negotiated. This is known as *forward exchange,* and the price for such transactions, which is fixed at the time the contract is made, is known as the *forward rate.* Rates for forward delivery can be quoted in the same way as spot rates; that is, the price of one currency is quoted in terms of another currency. More often, though, either currency is quoted in terms of its relation to the spot rate of the two currencies involved; that is, the forward rate is expressed as a discount from or premium on the spot rate. For example, if spot sterling is quoted in New York at $2·40 and the three-month forward rate at $2·3950, the three-month forward rate may be quoted as a 50-point (one-half cent) discount. Similarly, if the spot Deutsche mark (DM) is quoted at $0·25 and the six-month forward rate at $0·2525, the six-month forward rate may be expressed as a 25-point (one-quarter cent) premium. Forward rates are sometimes expressed also as a percentage deviation from the spot rate on a per annum basis. In the examples above, the discount on a per annum basis for three-month forward sterling is 0·833 per cent, while the premium on the six-month forward DM is 2·00 per cent.[2]

The spot market and the forward markets together make up the foreign-exchange market. There is a spot market for virtually every currency in the world. On the other hand, the number of currencies actively traded on the forward market is relatively small. Regular forward markets

2. For sterling, $4 \left(\dfrac{-0 \cdot 0050}{2 \cdot 40} \right) = -0 \cdot 00833$; for the DM $2 \left(\dfrac{0 \cdot 0025}{0 \cdot 25} \right)$ $= 0 \cdot 0200$

Note, of course, the forward discount on one currency is necessarily a forward premium on the other: for sterling holders, there is a premium on three-month forward dollars of 0·833 per cent; for holders of DMs, a discount on six-month forward dollars of 2·00 per cent.

exist only for the more widely traded currencies. Still, individual forward contracts may be negotiated for virtually any currency. They can be arranged through the country whose currency is traded, since most countries maintain some kind of forward market between their own currency and the United States dollar, the most widely traded currency of all.

Forward markets are useful to foreign traders and investors because they offer a comparatively inexpensive means of protecting their current operations against the risks involved in fluctuations of the spot rate. Many exchange transactions are based on the expectation of payments or receipts arising from future commercial or financial activities. With spot rates subject to variation, transactors assume an 'exchange risk' if they allow themselves to remain in an 'open' position of net current claims or net liabilities in a foreign currency. An excess of claims over liabilities is called a 'long position'; an excess of debts over claims, a 'short position'. The risk of a long position is that the spot price of the foreign currency may depreciate. It can be eliminated by selling forward anticipated foreign-exchange receipts. Conversely, the risk of a short position, appreciation of the spot rate, can be eliminated by buying forward to meet anticipated payment obligations. This is known as the process of *covering*. It is essentially a way of eliminating the uncertainty of the foreign-exchange element from individual international transactions.

In a similar fashion, forward markets offer a means of protecting the value of capital assets against exchange fluctuations. This is known as the process of *hedging*. Holders of assets denominated in a foreign currency can hedge against the possibility of depreciation by selling the currency forward. This ensures that the value of their assets will be maintained in terms of their own currency even if the value of the foreign currency should happen to drop. The foreign asset may or may not have a fixed date of maturity. Indeed, even non-liquid assets such as industrial plants owned abroad can be protected by selling forward foreign exchange equal to the nominal value of the asset. Moreover, such protection can be continually renewed so long as doubts about the foreign currency's price persist. But it should be observed that if forward exchange is selling at a discount, such accommodation may become quite expensive, even apart from transactions costs: if the spot rate does not in fact fall before the forward contract matures, the investor loses the difference between the spot rate and the price at which he sold forward. This is the cost of hedging (or covering).[3]

Speculation

The pure speculator in foreign exchange is an individual who has no other business or financial transactions in foreign exchange, but is merely interested in taking advantage of the possibility of changes in the spot rate of a currency over time. He is a deliberate risk-taker. Most operators in the foreign-exchange market, traders and investors alike, are more cautious; in general, they are risk-avoiders. They seek to eliminate the uncertainty of foreign-exchange transactions by covering an open position in a foreign currency. The speculator, on the other hand, is quite willing to assume an open position in a foreign currency, deliberately exposing himself to exchange risk in so far as his own view of the spot rate in the future differs from the over-all market expectation. He will make a profit on his activities to the extent that his own expectation is the more accurate. He loses money, of course, if he is wrong.

A 'bull' on a currency is a speculator who takes a more optimistic view than the market concerning the prospects for the price of the currency, while a 'bear' is a speculator who takes the opposite view. Speculation can take place in

3. Hedging differs fundamentally from covering in one important respect: whereas covering closes an open foreign-exchange position, hedging creates one. To put it differently, covering aims at eliminating exchange risk whereas hedging aims deliberately at incurring an exchange risk in order to offset an even greater exchange risk in the opposite direction.

either the spot or forward market. In the spot market a bull on sterling, for example, can buy spot sterling long in anticipation of reselling it later at a higher rate. A bear on sterling, on the other hand, can sell sterling short, borrowing pounds for sales in the spot market with the expectation that he will be able to repurchase sterling at a much lower price before his sterling loan falls due. Both of these transactions, however, involve costs which are additional to speculative risks, since the speculator must actually hold assets in foreign currencies if he is to gain from rate changes through purchase and sales of spot exchange. The bull must forgo interest earnings if he is to make an immediate outlay of his currency, the bear must incur interest costs if he is to borrow pounds for immediate sale. Thus, not only exchange-rate considerations but also the relevant interest rates tend to influence the speculator's decisions when he operates in the spot market.

By contrast, when he operates in the forward market the speculator can ignore these considerations, for here he can bet on a change in the price of a currency without committing any funds at all (unless a margin is required on forward contracts). The extra costs of speculation can be avoided. With the three-month forward rate at $2·3950, for example, a bull on sterling can buy pounds forward, with no immediate outlay of foreign exchange, and if he is correct, will be able to sell his pounds in the spot market at the end of three months, collecting the difference between the going market rate and $2·3950. If he is wrong, and sterling falls below $2·3950, he will of course receive less from his spot sale than he had to pay for the forward purchase. Similarly, a bear on sterling will sell pounds forward and, after three months, will gain or lose depending on his ability to guess the exchange-rate trend.

Clearly, from the speculator's point of view, the forward market is a far better vehicle for his purposes than the spot market. And it does seem to be true that the forward market is especially susceptible to speculative influences, even though banks as a rule do not like to accommodate purely speculative transactions. They generally prefer that their customers' transactions be for the purpose of avoiding exchange risk rather than for the purpose of undertaking it. This attitude does not necessarily rule out purely speculative transactions, but it does considerably diminish their importance. On the other hand, it does nothing to prevent occasional speculative behaviour by individuals – and even banks – who regularly use the forward market for non-speculative purposes. To give one prominent example: international traders are often tempted for the same reasons as pure speculators to assume a short position in a potentially weak currency. Often they will decline to cover future liabilities in a currency or refuse to sell forward their anticipated foreign-exchange earnings. The effect is the same as with pure speculation: forward demand for the currency declines relative to the forward supply. This behaviour is described as 'merchant speculation', and in volume terms represents today possibly an even more important source of speculative pressures in the foreign-exchange markets than so-called pure speculation.

In some respects the regular forward activities of banks themselves might be viewed as an additional source of speculative pressures in the foreign-exchange market, since banks rarely balance their forward sales exactly with an equivalent amount of forward purchases. Usually their forward-exchange position is as open as any speculator's. But this is not often the result of a deliberate decision to bet against general market trends. Rather, banks function in the foreign-exchange market as 'professional risk-bearers'. They 'make' the market, and in this sense their forward-exchange positions are thrust upon them by others. It is true, of course, that banks can adjust for the risks they assume by varying the rates at which they offer to buy and sell forward. But it is also true that if the banks were unwilling to assume any of these risks that the non-bank public prefers to avoid, even greater fluctuations of forward rates would undoubtedly ensue. It would be inappropriate, therefore, to describe *ordinary* bank behaviour as speculative.

Arbitrage

The exchange arbitrageur is an individual who is interested in taking advantage of differences in the price of a currency in separate markets at a single point of time.[4] His role is a vital one in the foreign-exchange markets. In effect, he provides the mechanism whereby geographically distinct exchange markets are integrated in an economic sense. Suppose, for instance, the price of sterling is $2.41 in London and $2.39 in New York. Arbitrageurs have an incentive to buy pounds in New York and sell them in London. Demand will increase in New York and supply in London until a single price prevails in the two locations. In fact, operations of this kind are universal in the currency markets, because money is the most homogeneous of commodities and because the costs of arbitrage are very small in relation to the amounts of money that may be traded. Furthermore, the element of time is practically eliminated through the speed of cable transfers. As a result, foreign-exchange markets around the world are, except where exchange controls or other market imperfections interfere, fully united by the activities of arbitrageurs.

Exchange arbitrage can take place in either the spot or forward market. Two-point arbitrage is that in which the arbitrageur finds a spread in the (spot or forward) rate of exchange between two currencies in two separate markets and acts so as to profit from it. Three-point (triangular) arbitrage is that in which the arbitrageur takes advantage of an inequality in the cross-rates among three currencies in three separate markets;[5] four-point arbitrage involves

4. Note the contrast with the speculator, who is interested in taking advantage of differences in the price of a currency in a single market at different points of time.

5. For example, suppose that the price of the pound sterling in terms of dollars ($/£) = 2·40 and in terms of Deutsche marks (DM/£) = 9·60.

four currencies and four markets; and even more complicated opportunities are conceivable. But no matter how
complicated his operations, the arbitrageur need never take
any risks. Except for the matter of moments required to
consummate his transactions, he need never assume an
open position in foreign exchange. He makes his profit
simply from engaging in simultaneous purchases and sales
of foreign currencies, a series of transactions in the course
of which he ends in the same currency with which he started.
He may also, occasionally, see an opportunity to add to his
profit by speculating as well on a possible change in the
exchange rate. But this is not integral to his arbitrage operations. By definition, the arbitrageur *qua* arbitrageur is no
speculator.

An interesting variant of exchange arbitrage is the operation known as *interest arbitrage*. This operation, too, plays
a vital integrative role: it serves to link physically separate
national financial markets and to promote their unity.
Interest arbitrageurs accomplish this result in the process
of taking advantage of international differences in the interest rates on comparable assets. For example, assume that
the (per annum) rate on three-month Treasury Bills today
is 5 per cent in London and only 3 per cent in New York.
American investors holding liquid assets have an incentive
to shift their funds to London: they will buy spot pounds
and invest them in British bills. At the same time, though,
they have an incentive to cover forward, for should the spot
rate of sterling depreciate before their investments mature,
their interest-arbitrage gains (measured in dollars) will be
diminished or perhaps even wiped out by an exchange loss.
To avoid this exchange risk, they will simultaneously sell
forward pounds, with the maturity of each forward contract set for the date the corresponding investment will

The price of the dollar in terms of marks (DM/$) must then be
$(DM/£)/($/£) = 4 \cdot 00$ for the cross-rates to be consistent. If (DM/$)
is anything else, say $5 \cdot 00$, arbitrageurs can profit by purchasing dollars
via the pound sterling for DM $4 \cdot 00$ and reselling for DM $5 \cdot 00$.
(Grubel, 1966, ch. 3).

mature. The forward contract determines the exchange rate at which both interest and principal are to be returned to the United States. Exchange-rate fluctuations cannot affect the investment return.

The forward contract also determines the cost of the interest-arbitrage operation – measured by the spread between the spot and forward-exchange rates. This spread represents an implicit interest rate on the use of forward exchange. Suppose that in the above illustration three-month forward pounds are selling at $0·6$ cents less than spot pounds. If the spot rate is at par ($\$2·40$), this amounts to a discount of $0·25$ per cent from the spot rate, or the equivalent of one per cent per annum rate of interest when expressed as a percentage deviation from the spot rate on an annual basis.[6] For the American arbitrageur, who needs to sell forward sterling, this represents a cost that he must subtract from the two per cent per annum interest differential in calculating the net return on his investment. Clearly, so long as the implicit interest rate is smaller than the explicit interest differential, the American will continue to have an incentive to shift funds to London. There is said to be an 'intrinsic premium' on sterling (an 'intrinsic discount' on the U.S. dollar). Should, however, the actual discount on forward sterling grow to as much as $1·2$ cents, which is an implicit interest rate of 2 per cent on an annual basis, the intrinsic premium on sterling will disappear. The arbitrage incentive ceases. And should the discount on forward sterling in fact widen beyond the difference in interest rates, a reverse incentive will emerge: British arbitrageurs will be encouraged to shift funds to New York, despite the attractive yield of bills in London, because of the even greater premium that can be earned on forward sales of dollars. There is said to be an 'intrinsic discount' on sterling (an 'intrinsic premium' on the dollar).

These relationships may be summarized algebraically.

6. The complete calculation is $\dfrac{2·394 - 2·400}{2·400} \times \dfrac{360}{90} = -0·01 = -1·0$ per cent. Cf. footnote 2.

Suppose R_d and R_f are the domestic and foreign per-annum interest rates on 'equivalent' securities, X_t is the forward price of the foreign currency (expressed in terms of the number of units of the domestic currency per unit of the foreign currency), X_o is the spot price of the foreign currency (expressed similarly), and T is time to maturity of the forward contract (expressed in days). In general, domestic investment funds will flow outward into foreign securities whenever there is an intrinsic premium on the foreign currency, i.e. whenever

$$R_d - R_f > \left[(X_t - X_o) / X_o \right] \frac{360}{T}.$$

The flow of funds will be inward whenever the inequality is reversed and there is an intrinsic discount on the foreign currency, i.e. whenever

$$R_d - R_f < \left[(X_t - X_o) / X_o \right] \frac{360}{T}.$$

No funds will flow whenever the explicit interest differential is just equal to the implicit interest rate on the use of forward exchange, i.e. whenever

$$R_d - R_f = \left[(X_t - X_o) / X_o \right] \frac{360}{T}.$$

This is the condition of arbitrage equilibrium. It is known as *interest parity*.[7] It illustrates that there is an intimate rela-

7. Actually, the precise condition of interest parity is the following:

$$\frac{R_d - R_f}{1 + R_f} = \left[(X_t - X_o) / X_o \right] \frac{360}{T}.$$

See Grubel, 1966, p. 9. However, for most purposes, unless R_f is excessively large, the equation can be reduced to the simpler formulation used in the text. The reader can check his understanding of the algebraic presentation of interest parity by substituting into it the numerical values assumed in the example of the previous paragraph. Either the U.S. or the U.K. may be taken to be the home country; it works both ways. Funds flow to London in this example whenever the implicit interest

tionship between the forward discount or premium on one currency in terms of another, and the difference in interest rates prevailing in the two countries. The forward exchange rate is said to be at 'interest parity' whenever the interest differential and forward discount or premium are equal. And indeed there is a clear tendency for parity to be established. The force that established this tendency, obviously, is arbitrage itself.

For example, suppose there is an intrinsic discount on sterling, the actual forward discount being greater than the interest differential in favour of London. In response to the incentive to move their short-term funds to New York, interest arbitrageurs will bid up the spot dollar price and bid down the forward rate, and as a result the forward premium on the dollar will narrow towards equality with the difference in interest rates. A distinct tendency toward interest parity will be established. This is the usual way in which parity is established, the forward spread adjusting to the international interest differential. But if the movement of funds across borders is large enough, the interest differential itself may be affected; the relationship between the difference in interest rates and forward discount or premium on forward exchange in fact is mutual. Once again, this emphasizes the vital role played by interest arbitrageurs in uniting currency and financial markets that are spatially distinct.

Interest arbitrageurs play a vital role as well in uniting currency and financial markets that are *temporally* distinct. By establishing simultaneous equilibrium in all forward markets, interest arbitrageurs provide the mechanism whereby the spot and various forward markets are made one in an economic sense. They usually accomplish this by means of the customary form of interest arbitrage involving

rate on the use of forward exchange is less than the 2 per cent explicit interest differential (an intrinsic premium on sterling, an intrinsic discount on the dollar); funds flow to New York whenever the implicit interest rate is greater than 2 per cent (an intrinsic discount on sterling, an intrinsic premium on the dollar).

a spot purchase and simultaneous forward sale of a currency. However, in addition they can accomplish this by means of a more unusual form of interest arbitrage involving a swap between two forward markets with different maturities (Sohmen, 1966, pp. 23–4). For example, an American investor might simultaneously purchase sterling three-months forward and sell six-months forward, at the same time lending pounds in London for three months and investing in British bills for six months. At no time is the investor's position in foreign exchange open: for the first three months his net foreign-exchange position is zero; for the next three months, he acquires a position in pounds sterling which is fully covered. Therefore, this is a pure arbitrage operation, and it reinforces the important integrative influence of the more customary form of interest arbitrage.[8]

The integrative influence of interest arbitrageurs is further reinforced by the activities of another category of transactors known as *trader arbitrageurs*. Interest arbitrageurs are 'owner arbitrageurs' – individuals, corporations, and banks who own the liquid funds they invest. Trader arbitrageurs, by contrast, are 'borrower arbitrageurs': they

8. Occasionally, an investor might prefer to take advantage of discrepancies between forward margins for different maturities of a currency without simultaneously undertaking to borrow and invest in the foreign financial market. That is, he might prefer simply to hold short positions in certain maturities against long positions in other maturities. Paul Einzig has described this as 'time arbitrage' (Einzig, 1966, ch. 7). However, this is not strictly a pure arbitrage operation analogous to the operation described in the text. True, in this case the operator can keep his over-all position in the currency concerned evenly balanced; in that sense the operation is more like arbitrage than speculation. But even if his over-all position is evenly balanced, the operator still incurs speculative risks, since technically a purchase of one maturity and a sale of another are independent transactions: the gain or loss from one transaction in no way depends on the gain or loss from the other. Indeed, since in a literal sense essentially different currencies are involved (i.e. the same currency differing in the essential respect of time of delivery), one might argue that the operation should more accurately be labelled 'double-barrelled speculation' (Grubel, 1966, p. 55).

borrow spot funds in a foreign country and purchase forward currency in order to cover the exchange risk. Unlike interest arbitrageurs, who are engaged in a purely financial operation, borrower arbitageurs are usually businessmen having to finance their trade. An importer, for instance, may be required to pay immediately for his purchases, even though he does not expect any receipts from his domestic sales until some time in the future. He must take out a loan now, to be repaid when his goods are sold. He faces two choices: he can either borrow at home and purchase the needed foreign currency spot; or he can borrow abroad and cover forward to the date when the loan repayment is due. His decision is a function of the same four variables which influence the decisions of interest arbitrageurs: the two interest rates and the spot and forward exchange rates. In other words, he too compares the interest-rate differential and the forward spread, and acts accordingly. His operations also have the same effects as those of professional interest arbitrageurs.

For example, an intrinsic discount on sterling will induce American and British importers to shift the locale of their trade financing from New York to London. These shifts are part of the 'leads and lags' in commercial payments: by switching their financing and covering forward, American importers delay ('lag') their payments of sterling, while British importers accelerate ('lead') their payments of dollars.[9] Like pure financial arbitrage, this constitutes a new outflow of short-term funds from London to New York. And like pure financial arbitrage, it establishes a distinct tendency toward interest parity, as the spot dollar price is bid up, the forward rate is bid down, and perhaps the interest differential itself is narrowed.

9. The 'leads and lags' also include examples of speculative behaviour, such as the following: U.K. exporters who delay their conversion of dollar earnings; U.S. exporters expecting payment in sterling, who speed up collection or even insist on sight terms; U.S. importers who run down inventories; and U.K. importers who build up their inventories.

How meaningful is the concept of interest parity? How true is it in the actual world that the forward discount or premium and the interest-rate differential between financial centres are mutually determined and tend to remain close? In theory, the relationship is intimate. In practice, however, the relationship tends to be weakened by a number of factors. In the first place, it must be noted that arbitrage requires broad and active markets in both short-term financial instruments and forward exchange. The national money market must provide a choice among assets as well as liquidity, and the market for the national currency must be capable of absorbing spot and forward sales and purchases without prices moving sharply. The nations whose financial and exchange markets can fulfil both of these requirements are few, being essentially the United States, Canada, Britain and a few of the continental European countries. For other countries financial and exchange markets are generally too thin to ensure a regular tendency toward interest parity. Moreover, even in the broader markets there are imperfections. For arbitrage to keep exchange rates and interst rates near parity, there must be a sufficiently large flow of funds. But often the necessary funds are lacking, owing either to legal complications on international transactions, or to transaction costs, or to ignorance of opportunities on the part of investors and traders. Deviation of rates from parity, consequently, can persist for quite long periods even among the major financial centres.

For that matter, deviations would probably persist even if sufficient funds happened to be available for foreign investment. Modern portfolio theory teaches that an investor's behaviour is a function not only of the expected rates of return on alternative assets, but also of the risk entailed by his actions. And investors generally associate a relatively high risk with all international transactions. Exchange risk, of course, can be covered. But there are other risks that cannot be covered – specifically, the risks of expropriation or inconvertibility. Because of these, investors responding to arbitrage incentive prefer to be somewhat cautious, adding foreign assets to domestic portfolios in a continuous, smooth fashion rather than abruptly. There exist no critical covered-earnings margins at which large amounts of funds will suddenly be shifted abroad. And this, in turn, implies that prolonged deviations of rates from parity would be highly probable even if investor knowledge were perfect and legal complications were absent (Grubel, 1966, pp. 12–17).

Finally, it must be observed that each financial market is characterized by not one but rather by a collection of interest rates. The multiplicity of rates gives rise to a number of relevant differentials, based on the many possible combinations open to the arbitrageur and on the market's assessment of the comparability of the rates involved. Determining the direction of net arbitrage incentives, therefore, is a highly complex matter. At any one time there are probably numerous arbitrage flows moving together. Indeed, there may even be two-way flows, since any particular forward-exchange spread may easily be compatible with the simultaneous existence of significant arbitrage incentives in both directions.

In recent years, the complexity of arbitrage calculations has been, if anything, heightened by the development of an entirely new kind of financial market – the foreign-currency deposit market, commonly called the Euro-currency system (Einzig, 1964). This is an interbank market for deposits denominated in some currency other than that of the country in which they are deposited; the single most important currency in the market is the United States dollar. Since its origin in the mid-1950s, the Euro-currency system has rapidly expanded into a fully-fledged international money market with its own structure of international interest rates which is quite distinct from national interest-rate structures. In turn, this has created ample additional scope for arbitrage by further increasing the number of relevant differentials, not only between the various international interest rates on deposits of different denomination, but also between these and the various national interest rates on comparable assets. Determining the direction of net arbitrage incentives has become more difficult than ever before.

Balance-of-payments stabilization

Speculation and arbitrage play an important role in the process of balance-of-payments adjustment. The problem of adjustment, we noted tentatively in chapter 1, is to reconcile differences between autonomous demand and supply of foreign exchange at a given exchange rate. (The notions of equilibrium and adjustment are more fully discussed in chapter 3.) Such differences are hardly unusual in a dynamic market, where conditions are constantly changing. Indeed, in a short-run sense such differences are occurring all the time. Only comparatively rarely, though, do they lead to longer-run payments difficulties of any consequence, for in most cases arbitrage and speculation function almost automatically to offset temporary discrepancies between the demand and supply of foreign exchange, and hence to stabilize the balance of payments. This is not necessarily the deliberate intention of arbitrageurs or speculators; it just happens to be incidental to their principal goal, which of course is to make a profit. Their effect is to promote payments stability: temporary pressures on the exchange rate are eliminated by movements of short-term capital in the foreign-exchange market.

For example, suppose a sudden excess of payments over receipts causes a deficit in the British balance of payments and a decline in the spot rate for the pound. If speculators are convinced that the deficit is temporary, they may purchase spot pounds in anticipation of a future rise in the price. This generates an immediate inflow of short-term capital – that is, an increased demand for sterling directly offsetting the initial excess supply and supporting the exchange rate. Alternatively, speculators may purchase sterling forward. In fact, this is their more probable course, since (as we have said) the extra interest costs of speculation can be avoided in the forward market. True, when speculators operate in the forward market, they have no need to move any funds immediately into sterling; they therefore provide no direct offset to the excess supply of pounds. But they do provide an indirect offset, by encouraging appropriate movements of arbitrage funds. Forward purchases of sterling push up the forward rate for sterling. This is assuming that the forward rate had previously been at interest parity *vis-à-vis* the dollar. With the spot rate already lower, an intrinsic premium on the pound is now created. Interest arbitrageurs are given a distinct incentive to shift their funds to London, and trader arbitrageurs a comparable incentive to shift the locale of their trade financing to New York. The joint effect of their operations will be an immediate inflow of short-term capital into Britain, supporting the spot rate of sterling and eliminating the deficit.

In the same way, a temporary excess of receipts over payments will be offset by an immediate outflow of funds, as speculators sell the pound spot or, alternatively, as they sell sterling forward and arbitrageurs respond to the intrinsic discount that is created.

Thus in numerous cases the foreign-exchange market is quite capable, in effect, of managing itself. Short-term capital movements, flowing in response to arbitrage or speculative incentives, function efficiently to eliminate downward as well as upward pressures on the exchange rate. This is precisely how the balance-of-payments adjusts to small or temporary discrepancies between the demand and supply of foreign exchange. Unfortunately, not all disequilibria are so small or temporary. Many are simply too large or enduring to be offset at the given exchange rate by flows of private funds. In such instances, the market may not be able to manage itself without difficulties. Official intervention may be necessary. Whether, when and how the financial authorities should intervene is a matter for further discussion.

In some instances, disequilibria may be so large or enduring that at the given exchange rate capital movements actually begin to destabilize the balance of payments rather than to stabilize it. They become 'perverse'. To illustrate, suppose that in the first example above speculators had been convinced not that the British deficit was temporary but rather that it signified an irreversible adverse shift of either the demand or supply schedule of sterling. Anticipating a further decline in the price of the pound, they would sell sterling spot, generating an outflow instead of an inflow of short-term capital to London. Additionally, they would sell sterling forward, encouraging an outward instead of an inward movement of arbitrage funds by creating an intrinsic discount on the pound. Together, these operations would add to the pressures on the spot rate of sterling and magnify the payments deficit. Events like these occur. When they do, and when for other reasons it is desired to maintain the exchange rate at its current level or within a specified range, a particularly strong case may be made for official intervention in the exchange market.

The Financial Authorities

The foreign-exchange market comes as close to the perfectly competitive model of economic theory as any market can. The product is homogeneous, in that foreign currency purchased from one seller is the same as foreign currency purchased from another. Participants in the market have nearly perfect knowledge, since it is easy to obtain exchange-rate quotations from alternative sources in a short period of time. And there are large numbers of buyers and sellers. Yet the foreign-exchange market is by no means a free market. Within the context of their over-all balance-of-payments policy, the financial authorities of each nation can – and, in practice, do – intervene directly to restrict competition in two essential respects: (a) they limit entry into the market; and (b) they limit movements of the market price.

Limitations on entry

A first condition for the functioning of the exchange market is *convertibility*. There can be no transfers of purchasing power between countries unless in fact the different national currencies can be exchanged for one another. A fully convertible currency is one that can be bought and sold freely at the prevailing price, regardless of the residence or purposes of transactors.[10] Before the international financial collapse of the 1930s, virtually all currencies were fully convertible in this sense (except during and immediately after World War I). Today only a handful can be bought and sold freely – including, most prominently, the United States and Canadian dollars, the Deutsche mark, and the Swiss franc. For the many others there remain still, more than two decades after the end of the Second World War, exchange controls of various kinds limiting entry into the market to certain types of transactors or to certain types of transactions. Such is the legacy of the interwar period and the Second World War.

The essence of exchange control is rationing. In its most extreme form, the government assumes a complete monopoly of foreign exchange. There can be no legitimate free market for the national currency, though there may well be an illegitimate (black) market in which the currency is bought and sold illegally. The currency is made totally inconvertible. Local residents are required to surrender all foreign-exchange earnings to the financial authorities. In turn, residents wishing to make payments of foreign exchange must obtain it from the authorities who, since market criteria are abrogated, may allocate the foreign currency available to them simply under terms of their own choosing. Discrimination can hardly be avoided under such circumstances. Discrimination may be in favour of certain types of

10. In the days of the gold standard, convertibility was defined more broadly to refer to a currency that could be freely exchanged for *gold* at the prevailing price. Today, only the United States dollar is convertible in this old-fashioned sense, and then only at the intercentral-bank level.

transactors or certain types of transactions, or it may be in favour of certain countries.

A particularly interesting method of discrimination is through multiple exchange rates. When a currency is totally inconvertible, the government can buy and sell foreign exchange at quite different rates if it so chooses. Usually, governments choose to differentiate even among buying rates and selling rates, in order to be able to discriminate as widely as possible according to the sources and anticipated uses of foreign exchange. Alternatively, governments can effectively discriminate by creating an unrestricted exchange market for certain purposes. That is, they can partially free the local currency from exchange control. By requiring that only the foreign exchange earned from (needed for) designated transactions be surrendered to (obtained from) official agencies at fixed rates, and by permitting the remaining exchange to be bought and sold freely at rates determined by private supply and demand, the authorities can ensure that certain types of transactions and transactors will be encouraged and others discouraged.

One of the objectives of the International Monetary Fund (I.M.F.), when it was created at Bretton Woods in 1944, was to re-establish a system of multilateral international payments free of such discriminatory currency practices. The famous Article VIII of the I.M.F. Charter obliged member-countries to remove as soon as possible all restrictions on payments for current transactions. Residents were to be permitted to purchase foreign exchange freely for the purpose of acquiring imports, and non-residents earning local currency through sales of goods and services were to be permitted to convert it without limit into foreign currencies. The Articles of Agreement did not require convertibility for transactions of a capital nature; the means for attaining that objective were left entirely to the discretion of the members. In fact, most countries have procrastinated in this respect: the overwhelming majority still regulate transfers of capital across their borders. Residents are forbidden to purchase foreign exchange for the purpose of acquiring certain types of assets abroad without special permission, and non-residents are restricted in their right to convert into foreign currencies local currency earned through sales of capital assets.

For that matter, even with respect to the objective of current-account convertibility there have been delays, as most countries have availed themselves of the escape clause implied by the postwar 'transitional period' mentioned in Article IX of the Charter. Initially, this transitional period was expected to end in 1952. Fifteen years later, however, in late 1967, only thirty-one of the Fund's one hundred and six members had as yet met their original obligations under Article VIII. This is quite a small number, although it is true that it includes practically all of the major financial and industrial powers. This means that probably most international transactions today are conducted in currencies that are convertible for current purposes and, in a few instances (the handful mentioned above), for capital purposes as well. Nevertheless, it is significant that so many countries continue to limit entry into the foreign-exchange market. Some of their currencies are 'externally convertible' only – that is, convertible only by non-residents. Others are 'internally convertible' as well – that is, also convertible by residents – but not for all purposes. Most commonly, these currencies are externally convertible only, and only for current transactions. This is the absolute minimum necessary to foster multilateral international trade.

It is necessary to explain the longevity and pervasiveness of exchange controls, and also to discover why they are still used by so many countries. Essentially, it is because their immediate effects are relatively certain. Governments confronted by an excess demand for foreign exchange can by administrative fiat directly restrict certain or all foreign expenditures to whatever level is desired at the given exchange rate. Thus in the short run at least exchange controls are a more effective instrument for managing the foreign-exchange market than most of the policy alternatives that might be considered. What governments tend to neglect, however, is the fact that these effects on the balance of payments may not be lasting. Exchange controls operate by suspending the free market: they do not eliminate the excess demand for foreign exchange, they merely suppress it. In the longer run, therefore, so long as the restrictions are less than absolute, outlets will be sought for that excess demand, in much the same manner – to evoke the classic simile – as water seeks its own level. Smart operators can be expected sooner or later to devise and attempt new methods of circumventing the government's authority, and as they do the effectiveness of existing regulations is bound to decline. Moreover, exchange controls invite retaliation in kind, so that over time their impact may well be nullified by similar actions of other governments. And finally, it must be noted that exchange controls do inevitably influence the allocative efficiency of the domestic economy, usually – though not necessarily always – negatively. The balance-of-payments effectiveness of exchange control is not purchased without a cost. We shall have more to say on these matters in chapter 3.

Limitations on price movements

Governments also limit movements of the price in the foreign-exchange market. The spot rate of exchange is not allowed to fluctuate freely in response to variations of demand and supply. When the I.M.F. was created, another of its objectives was to re-establish a system of relatively stable rates free of the confusion and competitive depreciation of the 1930s. The negotiators at Bretton Woods were convinced that a régime of uncontrolled exchange rates would be undesirable. It was thought that not only would there be considerable exchange risks discouraging to trade and investment but such a system would probably also generate destabilizing rather than stabilizing flows of speculative and arbitrage funds. Therefore, it was agreed that rates should be officially pegged. The rules would not permit sustained appreciations or depreciations of any currency in the market. At the same time, though, it was

thought that rates should not be immutable. Some element
of flexibility would be necessary to ensure against distor-
tions in the rate structure. Hence it was also agreed that
each member-country could, under appropriate circumstances and with the concurrence of the I.M.F., occasionally
shift its official peg to a new level. The rule would permit
once-for-all devaluations or revaluations of currencies.

Thus was the Bretton Woods exchange system born – an
attempt to achieve the advantages of rate stability without
the disadvantages of rate rigidity. As such it was a com-
promise, and like most compromises it has been subject to
a crossfire of critique and criticism. The arguments for and
against the system will not be assessed here; that is more
properly the province of another of the volumes in this
series. For the purposes of this volume it is sufficient simply
to note that whatever its faults or virtues, the Bretton Woods
system happens to be currently the institutional framework
within which official balance-of-payments policy around the
world must try to operate.

Under the system each country is obliged to declare a par
value for its currency and to ensure that spot exchange
transactions take place at rates based on this value within
margins differing from parity by no more than one per
cent in either direction.[11] Margins are enforced by official
intervention to offset discrepancies between demand and
supply in the market. Downward or upward pressures on
the exchange rate that for one reason or another are not
contained by movements of private short-term capital must
be contained by movements of official short-term capital.
In effect, each government is obliged to function as residual buyer and seller of its own currency. When the balance
of payments is in deficit and the price of the national

11. In fact, the maxima and minima for exchange transactions have
been set even closer to the peg: spot rates are presently allowed to differ
from parity by only some 0·75 per cent in most cases – a total spread of
just 1·5 per cent. The only significant exception is Switzerland – not a
member of the I.M.F. – which maintains margins of two per cent in
either direction.

currency declines, the authorities must buy; when payments are in surplus and the price rises, they must sell. This is how the foreign-exchange market is managed today.

Within this context, of course, it is quite possible for the authorities of a country to fashion intervention policies which differ sharply from those of another and even from previous policies of its own. The international rules do not require uniformity of actual practice. Thus some governments may allow the exchange rate to move within virtually the full range of the spread, intervening only at the limits or close to them. Others may intervene earlier, so as to affect the trend in the market or even to bring about a *de facto* stability at a level well within the limits of the spread. Some may even, if they wish, both buy and sell at parity itself. All these approaches, and variants of them, are possible under present arrangements.

Intervention in the spot market is financed out of a reserve stockpile of internationally acceptable assets. This suggests that governments must always be concerned about the adequacy of their monetary reserves. Theoretically there is no limit at all to how much of its own currency a government can sell; its currency is merely its IOU, and foreign exchange can be accumulated practically indefinitely. But there is a distinct limit to how much of its own currency a government can buy – a limit set by the size of its reserve stockpile plus its access to external credit facilities. Few countries, consequently, are likely to aim deliberately for a net deficit of external payments. Many countries, on the other hand, might be expected to aim for a net surplus (a net increase of reserves over time) in order to ensure themselves of adequate international liquidity in the event of unforeseen contingencies. As a result, the balance-of-payments targets of all countries taken together may very well add not to zero, as suggested in the last chapter, but rather to a quite substantial excess of surpluses over deficits – at the same time that, as we know, empirical measures of balance, which serve as the official target variables for most governments, tend collectively to add to a quite substantial excess of total deficits. The danger of conflict among national policies is thus probably even greater than it appeared in chapter 1.

By long tradition, gold is the most generally acceptable of all monetary reserve assets. However, gold is not particularly useful as a medium of intervention in the exchange market: the gold portion of official reserves is usually held as a store of value, not as a transactions balance. For transactions purposes governments prefer to hold United States dollars and British pounds sterling, the two currencies most widely traded by private participants in the market. The dollar market is the broadest currency exchange in the world, the sterling market is next. Developments in these markets *vis-à-vis* any one currency are quickly communicated to the markets for all other currencies as well. Operations in dollars or sterling, therefore, are more efficient than operations in any other international asset. This explains why the dollar and sterling occupy such a central role as reserve currencies in the international monetary system today.

Intervention in the forward market

Under the Bretton Woods system, the financial authorities may intervene to influence the rate not only for spot exchange transactions but also for forward transactions. For the latter, however, the international rules are less specific. According to Article IV of the I.M.F. Charter, the margin by which the price of forward exchange may differ from the spot price is not to be 'more than the Fund considers reasonable'. Since reasonableness is not defined, this means in fact that there are no legally fixed limits to the movements of forward exchange rates. Individual governments are free to choose whether to intervene in the forward market or not at their own discretion.

In fact, governments have chosen increasingly in recent years to intervene actively in the forward market. This is true, in particular, of the major financial powers. Because of its special susceptibility to speculative influences, the forward market is an important indicator of expectations with respect to spot rates. Frequently, a drop in the forward rate of a currency is the signal of a deterioration of market confidence in the current parity. If the decline is not reversed, it can easily lead to a cumulative wave of adverse speculation generating outflows of short-term capital directly as well as indirectly via the creation of 'perverse' arbitrage incentives. To prevent developments of this sort, national authorities today are more willing then ever before to limit movements of forward exchange rates. They do so, most commonly, by functioning as residual buyer and seller of their own currency in the forward market.[12] The analogy with the principle of intervention in the spot market is perfect.

Intervention in the forward market can be advantageous to the authorities. Consider once again the example of a sudden deficit in the British balance of payments, and assume that speculators are convinced in this instance that devaluation of sterling is inevitable. They will sell pounds both spot and forward. The international rules require the British authorities to support the spot price of sterling; the forward rate, though, may be allowed to decline, creating an intrinsic discount on the pound.[13] Britain will lose dollar reserves through the spot market to both arbitrageurs and speculators. However, now suppose that the British authorities choose to support the forward price of sterling. By selling dollars forward they can prevent the emergence of a 'perverse' arbitrage incentive; if they so desire, they can even bring about an intrinsic premium that will generate

12. An alternative technique involves the use of swap accommodations: the authorities buy (sell) spot exchange at a certain rate while simultaneously selling (buying) forward exchange at another rate. The use of this technique, however, is not widespread.

13. For simplicity of exposition, again assume that the forward rate had previously been at interest parity *vis-à-vis* the dollar. We can therefore be quite certain that there is already an *explicit* discount on the pound: with British payments in deficit, London interest rates most probably are higher than New York interest rates, hence the forward rate of sterling may be assumed to be lower than the spot rate.

an inflow of short-term capital.[14] As a result, market confidence will be promoted and reserve losses cut, as pressures are deflected away from the spot market into the forward market. Indeed, reserves will actually be augmented over time, for as forward commitments mature, speculators will have to reverse their short positions by spot purchases of sterling at a spot rate for pounds greater than the price at which they contracted to sell pounds forward. The authorities will profit at the expense of speculators by an amount equal to the number of forward dollars sold to speculators multiplied by the difference between the (lower) original forward rate and the (higher) current spot rate.

On the other hand, suppose that in spite of the support given to the forward rate, the British do decide to devalue. In that event it is the speculators who gain, not the authorities. The government will lose an amount of dollars equal to the number of forward dollars sold to speculators multiplied by the difference between the original forward rate and the new current spot rate (which of course is lower). Intervention in the forward market can also be disadvantageous to the authorities.

Because of this disadvantage, most economists writing on the subject, while acknowledging the general merits of official forward intervention, in principle have opposed support of the forward rate whenever the authorities harbour some reservations about their ability or willingness to prevent a devaluation. Speculators, it is argued, should not be permitted to profit at the expense of the nation's taxpayers. But what if the government refrains from intervention in the forward market prior to a possible devaluation? R. Z. Aliber was the first analyst to note that the government is still exposed to a substantial financial loss, since speculators can sell sterling at the old spot rate and then return their funds after devaluation at the new, lower spot rate. The authorities must absorb the reflux of speculative

14. See the section on arbitrage in the first part of this chapter and especially the pages on interest arbitrage.

funds. They lose an amount of dollars equal to the number of dollars sold spot to speculators that do return, multiplied by the difference between the old and new spot rates. As Aliber pointed out, the relevant comparison is not between (a) the loss suffered by the authorities when first they support the forward rate and then devalue; and (b) no loss. The relevant comparison is between (a) and (c) the loss suffered when the authorities refrain from supporting the forward rate and then devalue. In Aliber's view, (c) is likely to exceed (a), primarily because of the stabilizing effects of forward intervention on market confidence. The authorities should therefore always support the forward rate, *even if* it appears that the parity might be changed (Aliber, 1962, 1963).

Many economists disagree, insisting still that forward intervention is imprudent when devaluation is a possibility.

This remains a controversial issue in the literature. A typical position is taken by H. N. Goldstein, who begins by restating Aliber's argument in a formally elegant fashion (Goldstein, 1966). Considering country Z, Goldstein identifies (a) the loss absorbed by the authorities when they first support the forward rate and then devalue, as $F(d/1+d)$, where F = the number of forward dollars sold by the authorities, and d = the percentage by which the devaluation of Z's currency, which he whimsically calls the zengo, increases the zengo price of the dollar.[15] Analogously, (c) the loss absorbed when the authorities refrain from supporting the forward rate and then devalue, is identified as $X(d/1+d)$, where X = the number of dollars sold to speculators through the spot market that eventually return at the new spot rate. The comparison is between $F(d/1+d)$ and

15. For simplicity, Goldstein assumes that the pre-devaluation exchange rate was one zengo = one dollar, so that after devaluation $z(1+d) = \$1$ or $z1 = \$1/(1+d)$. Therefore, the authorities must pay $(1+d)$ zengos for each spot dollar they buy to liquidate their maturing forward contracts; but for each dollar they deliver in honouring their commitments, the authorities receive only one zengo. Hence their loss, measured in zengos, is d/F; and since d/F zengos now equal $d/F/(1+d)$ dollars, their loss in dollars is $F(d/1+d)$.

X $(d/1+d)$. Since d is presumed to be identical in the two instances, Goldstein deduces that the crucial question posed by Aliber is whether $F \gtreqless X$. It is his opinion that $F < X$, since

The pressure to devalue will be greater in the absence of forward intervention. For one thing reserve losses will occur at an accelerated rate. For another the degree of fundamental imbalance is likely to seem more severe since the authorities will be less able to judge what part of their reserve losses stems from speculation and what part reflects their basic payments deficit. Thus the authorities may feel that their underlying position is worse than it really is and devalue at an early date . . . .

[On the other hand] if the authorities intervene, they will not be forced to the wall so soon and there will be a powerful temptation to delay a devaluation in the hope that 'something will turn up'. But, by hypothesis, nothing does. Thus the eventual adjustment in par values is likely to occur with speculators having larger short positions in the suspect currency than when the authorities do not support the forward rate. (Goldstein 1966 pp. 450, 454).

Goldstein therefore concludes that the authorities should refrain from supporting the forward rate when it appears that the parity might be changed. As indicated previously, this is a typical argument.

We must consider whether such a conclusion is justifiable. The answer is no, for two-counter-arguments can be raised. In the first place, Goldstein's conclusion depends on the assumption that d is identical in the two instances – that is, on the assumption 'that the hypothesized devaluation, if it occurs, will be of the same magnitude whether or not the authorities have outstanding forward commitments' (Goldstein, 1966, p. 454). Although adopted by many, this is a weak assumption. Goldstein's own reasoning, which is quite sensible, admits that the degree of fundamental payments imbalance is likely to seem more severe when the authorities refrain from forward-exchange intervention than when they do not. This not only suggests that they will probably devalue at an earlier date when they confine their operations to the spot market. It also suggests that they will probably devalue by a greater amount.

Secondly, it is necessary to ask whether the *probability* of devaluation is likely to be identical in the two instances, as Goldstein and others who share his position also implicitly assume. This too is a weak assumption. The authorities can rarely be absolutely certain about their ability or willingness to prevent a devaluation. Ideally the decision to devalue a currency should be based on an analysis of the real factors underlying the country's international economic position. In practice the decision tends to be taken in haste and under pressure. Inevitably, the ambiguity surrounding the causes of an external imbalance forces the government to rely on more inferential data – in particular, on the rate and magnitude of reserve losses. And we know that when the authorities refrain from forward intervention, reserve losses will occur at an accelerated rate. Again by Goldstein's own reasoning, this is apt to convince the authorities that their underlying payments situation is worse than it really is. They are therefore more likely to devalue under these circumstances than if they were to commit themselves from the beginning to support of the forward rate.

Thus the crucial question posed by Aliber is not simply whether $F \gtrless X$, as Goldstein deduces, or even whether $F(d/1+d) \gtrless X(d/1+d)$. Rather, it is whether the *expected value* of financial losses is greater if the authorities intervene to support the forward rate or if they do not – that is, whether:

$$p F(d/1 + d) \gtrless p' X(d'/1 + d'),$$

where p is the probability and d the magnitude of devaluation in the event of forward support; and p' is the probability and d' the magnitude of devaluation in the absence of forward support. Goldstein argues, probably correctly, that $F > X$. But it is also probably correct, as we have argued here, that $p < p'$ and $d < d'$. Therefore, it is impossible to assert *a priori* which of the two sides of the total expression is likely to be larger. The specific circumstances of the moment must be known before proper estimates of the several variables can be attempted. Ultimately, it is a matter of judgement for the authorities themselves to determine whether to intervene in the forward market or not. This is a decision that can only be taken within the context of the government's over-all balance-of-payments policy.

3 Balance-of-Payments Policy: Theory

Balance-of-payments policy is essentially a matter of means and ends. A range of policy instruments is available to the financial authorities for dealing with problems of payments imbalance. Likewise, a range of policy objectives is formulated by the authorities, which may or may not always be compatible with the achievement of external equilibrium. There are no set rules in these matters. The problem is to make the correct choices – that is, to allocate means to ends. The available instruments of policy must be evaluated for their potentiality, both in over-all quantitative terms and qualitatively in terms of their suitability for specific tasks. How effective are they, and how interchangeable in practice? It is also necessary to evaluate the costs associated with each instrument of policy. What are likely to be the alternative opportunities forgone when one particular goal is sought? Finally, it is necessary to make the allocation of means to ends in the hope of maximizing policy objectives at least cost. This kind of calculus is quite familiar to economic theorists; it is presumably what economics is all about, and it is certainly what the theory of balance-of-payments policy is all about.

The range of balance-of-payments policy instruments will be examined in the first section of this chapter. Particular attention will be paid to the consistency of external equilibrium with other economic objectives of government policy. The second part will, in turn, consider some of the more important factors influencing the choice between the various policy alternatives.

The Range of Policies

Adjustment

According to the theory of exchange rates, there are essentially two mechanisms of adjustment to an imbalance of international transactions. Assume an excess of *ex ante* payments over receipts. If the exchange rate is free to move, the price of foreign exchange will immediately be bid up and domestic money will depreciate. The gap between autonomous demand and supply of exchange will be closed by movements along the existing schedules to the point where they intersect. This is known as the exchange-rates approach to balance-of-payments adjustment. Alternatively, if the exchange-rate is pegged, the deficit will gradually reduce the net foreign liquidity of the country, siphoning off internal purchasing power as domestic money, on balance, is sold for foreign currencies. Actively circulating balances will be withdrawn from circulation, and as a result domestic prices and incomes will decline, eventually contracting autonomous demand for foreign exchange and possibly also expanding the supply. The gap between the two schedules will be closed as both of them shift until they intersect at the prevailing parity. Under the classical gold standard, when prices of goods and services were more flexible than they are today, most of the burden was borne by price changes. In the twentieth century, by contrast, most of the burden is borne instead by changes of employment and income. That is why this mechanism is known today as the effective-demand (or income) approach to balance-of-payments adjustment, although price changes do still play an important, albeit subsidiary, role in the process.'

These two adjustment mechanisms are both automatic. They describe how the private market will respond to a payments imbalance in the absence of overt official intervention (other than intervention to peg the rate of exchange). Income and price changes, generated either

1. This treatment is necessarily brief and superficial. The subject is treated more thoroughly in another of the volumes of this series.

directly (when the rate is pegged) or indirectly (via rate changes when pegging is absent), will compel a reallocation of resources[2] leading to shifts in the volume and direction of exports, imports, and autonomous international investments. This is what distinguishes the adjustment process. Balance-of-payments adjustment may be defined as a *marginal reallocation of productive resources and hence of exchanges of goods, services and investments under the influence of changes of relative prices, incomes and/or exchange rates*. Balance-of-payments adjustment policies are those which achieve external balance in this manner.

We must consider the range of balance-of-payments adjustment policies, and the specific ways in which the government can intervene overtly in the private-market adjustment process. Essentially, the authorities have two alternatives. They can either actively *reinforce* the automatic market response to a payments disturbance, or at least allow that response to operate by reacting passively, or they can *resist* it.

Once again, we may assume an excess of payments over receipts. If the authorities choose to reinforce the automatic market response, they can either (1) keep the exchange rate pegged and encourage the necessary price and income changes by means of *deflationary monetary and fiscal policies (financial policy)*,[3] or (2) hasten the exchange-rate change by *devaluation of the local currency*. These are the 'classical' adjustment methods. On the other hand, if they choose to resist the automatic market response, the authorities can adopt one of three additional options. (3) They can impose *restrictions* of various kinds – tariffs,

2. 'Reallocation of resources' should be understood to mean not only switches from one kind of employment to another, but also switches to and from a state of unemployment.

3. Monetary policy describes the use of variations in the quantity of money to raise or lower interest rates, tighten or ease monetary conditions, and hence indirectly lower or raise aggregate demand. Fiscal policy describes the use of taxation and expenditure policies by the government to raise or lower aggregate demand. Fiscal and monetary policy together are designated as financial policy.

quotas, etc. – on imports of goods and services, on capital outflows, and on government overseas expenditures. In addition, they can subsidize exports of goods and services or offer inducements for foreign capital inflows. The effect of such actions is to close the gap between the demand and supply schedules of foreign exchange by shifting the two curves until they intersect at the prevailing parity. (4) They can suspend convertibility and resort to *exchange controls*, rationing foreign exchange under terms of their own choosing. The existing schedules, the prevailing parity, and the payments gap all remain as before; the free market, however, is suspended. (5) They can *finance* the imbalance, either directly by selling spot exchange, or indirectly by intervening in the financial and exchange markets to induce inward movements of short-term capital. Again, the existing schedules and prevailing parity remain, but under this option the payments gap is closed by accommodating flows of public and/or private funds.

On the other hand, if receipts exceed payments, the authorities can choose the opposite of any of these alternatives: (1) inflationary financial policy; (2) exchange revaluation; (3) removal or relaxation of restrictions and subsidies; (4) removal or relaxation of exchange controls; or (5) financing, either by purchasing spot exchange or by inducing outward movements of short-term capital.

Thus, depending on whether payments are in deficit or surplus, the authorities have, in all, a total of five policy alternatives, two of which involve reinforcing the automatic market response, and three of which involve resisting it. Not all of these, though, represent genuine balance-of-payments adjustment policies. Financing should be excluded. Reserve movements or private short-term capital flows induced by official actions are merely accommodating, 'below-the-line' transactions, which can affect only the net foreign liquidity of the country; they cannot generate a reallocation of resources directly. Of course, they may do so indirectly, but only if the authorities permit the change of net foreign liquidity to have its full impact on internal purchasing power. However, if the authorities do permit this, then they are really selecting their first policy choice described above – financial policy reinforcing, actively or passively, the private-market adjustment process. The reason for financing an imbalance is precisely that it provides an alternative to that choice – an opportunity to resist the private-market adjustment process, at least temporarily, by means of simultaneously offsetting monetary and fiscal policies. This is what is meant by balance-of-payments *stabilization* (see chapter 2): the flows of funds fill the gap between external payments and receipts while leaving prices and incomes as they were before. By definition, this is not balance-of-payments *adjustment*.

On the other hand, the four remaining options do represent genuine balance-of-payments adjustment policies. They are all capable of achieving what is meant by adjustment. The two classical policies, both of which involve reinforcing the automatic market response to a disturbance, most certainly should be included. Similarly, we should include the two options involving resistance to the automatic market response. Restrictions and subsidies affecting trade and investment influence the allocation of resources directly, and so do exchange controls, even though in the first instance these latter leave prices, incomes, and exchange rates unaffected. The rationing of foreign exchange inevitably causes expenditure switches leading to shifts of resources and exchanges at the margin. In the broadest sense, therefore, everything except financing should be included in the range of adjustment policies available to the authorities for dealing with problems of payments imbalance.

If this is so, then the question arises as to whether there are any grounds for continuing to distinguish between those policies which resist the automatic market response and those which reinforce it. Many economists think that there are, for it is obvious that the resource reallocation generated by restrictions or exchange controls will not be the same as that generated by the classical adjustment methods. Many agree with Fritz Machlup that only the latter are

truly deserving of the title 'adjustment'. The former, Machlup argued in an important essay published in 1965 (see
Machlup, 1965a), are merely 'compensatory corrections'.
They do not achieve adjustment (in the classical sense);
they merely remove the *need* for adjustment, by generating
an alternative reallocation of resources. Hence they are not
'legitimate' (p. 206). They are incapable of 'full equilibration' (p. 188).[4]

It must be decided whether or not Machlup is correct
and whether the range of 'legitimate' adjustment policies
is restricted to the two classical mechanisms. The answer
depends on what is meant by 'full equilibration'.

Equilibrium

In economic analysis, the concept of equilibrium is a
methodological device employed in connexion with
'models' containing a number of variables connected by
certain stipulated relationships. Models vary greatly. The
number of variables may be few or many; the stipulated
relationships may be behavioural, institutional, or techno-
logical. Models are used to identify the causal nexus between different events or changes. The economist puts them
to work by introducing a change in an 'independent'
(exogenous) variable, and then observing how the disturbance subsequently affects the 'dependent' (endogenous)
variables acting upon one another according to the assumed
relationships. The series of reactions represents the process
of adjustment. The process is complete when all the variables in the model achieve a new state of mutual compatibility. This is equilibrium – 'a constellation of selected
interrelated variables so adjusted to one another that no

4. The pages noted in parentheses locate the quoted phrases. Subsequently, an effort was made to distinguish between three different
kinds of 'compensatory corrections'. These were 'real correctives',
which influence the international flow of goods and services; 'financial
correctives', which influence the international flow of investments;
and 'corrective management of government transactions', which
influences the balance of foreign payments on government account
(Fellner *et al.*, 1966, pp. 246–8).

inherent tendency to change prevails in the model which they constitute' (Machlup, 1958).

In international economic analysis, the concept of equilibrium is employed specifically with reference to the prevailing rate of exchange. We must consider whether the given rate is an equilibrium rate. For the analyst, the problem of defining equilibrium in international payments is a problem of identifying an equilibrium rate of exchange.

In chapter 1, balance-of-payments equilibrium was tentatively defined as an equality of autonomous transactions requiring foreign payments and autonomous transactions involving foreign receipts. This is the necessary condition: an equilibrium exchange rate must equate demand and supply of foreign exchange. But this is not a sufficient condition. To be sufficient, the rate must be specified in two additional respects. First, what is the length of the period over which demand and supply must be equated? And second, what is the relationship of the demand and supply of foreign exchange to other relevant variables?

(1) Time period. Since demand and supply are 'flow' concepts, an equilibrium exchange rate must be defined in terms of some specified time period.[5] Over a very short period – an hour, a day, even a week – demand and supply are hardly ever equal in a dynamic market, except by chance. And over a very long period – say, two or three decades – demand and supply can hardly remain unequal. This means that the time period over which demand and supply are to be equated should be long enough to even out the effects of self-correcting short-term disturbances of a daily, weekly, monthly, or seasonal nature. The minimum period must be

5. A time period can be specified only in an *ex ante* sense, i.e. only when the equilibrium concept is used for analytical purposes. A time period cannot be specified in an *ex post* sense, i.e. in the sense of describing a real historical situation; that would be 'misplaced concreteness' because of the general fallacy involved in jumping the distance between a useful general fiction and particular observed data. (Machlup, 1958, p. 122).

at least a year in length. At the same time the period should not be so long that it obscures really fundamental imbalances of payments. The maximum period cannot be longer than, at most, the duration of the average business cycle.

When considering the business cycle itself, should the minimum period be longer than a year, long enough to even out the effects of cyclical disturbances, too? Ragnar Nurkse, in his now classic essay on international monetary equilibrium, argued that it should, on the grounds that there are no essential differences between cyclical fluctuations and (say) seasonal fluctuations: both, he suggests, tend to be generally self-correcting. 'This would give a period of between five and ten years' (Nurkse, 1945). However, as a guide for analysis, this length of time seems quite excessive. In the first place, the duration of the average business cycle is uncertain, individual cycles frequently completing their course in something less than half a decade. And of greater importance, it is uncertain that cyclical fluctuations do in fact tend to be self-correcting. Cyclical changes need not cancel out. There are no *a priori* reasons for assuming that such variables as national income, international investment flows, etc. will remain unchanged over a period of several years – to say nothing of such parameters as tastes, technology, and factor endowments. On the contrary, there are good reasons for supposing that in most instances cyclical changes will fail to cancel out. Consequently, for analytical purposes it is appropriate to define the time period over which demand and supply are to be equated as no more than one year in length. Imbalances that endure beyond a year may be considered indicative of a disequilibrium exchange rate.

(2) Relationship to other variables. Equilibrium describes the mutual compatibility of *selected* inter-related variables in a theoretical model. However, in the real world ultimately *all* variables are inter-related. Therefore, while any particular set of variables may be quite compatible for the moment, if we add one more variable a situation of incom-

patibility may be created. The concept of equilibrium is relative. It all depends on which variables are included in the selected set, and which excluded.

Concerning the equilibrium exchange rate the selected set of variables includes, as a minimum, the demand and supply of foreign exchange (each related to the price of foreign exchange). These constitute the basic model. The analytical problem is whether to include, in addition, either or both of two additional variables that are of particular relevance in the balance-of-payments context. The first is the level of *restrictions,* the second is the level of *employment.*

Suppose, for example, that the supply of foreign exchange currently equals demand, but only because of the recent imposition of new trade or exchange restrictions or because existing restrictions have been intensified. Is this an equilibrium exchange rate? In the essay previously cited, Nurske indicated that it was not:

The answer is clearly in the negative. To use our definition properly, we must take the structure of trade barriers existing at a given starting point. If subsequently a certain exchange rate can be maintained, or a balance-of-payments deficit closed, only by means of an increase in trade barriers, then the rate cannot be accepted as the equilibrium rate. The true equilibrium rate is that rate at which payments and receipts are equalized without additional restrictions on trade. (Nurske, 1945, p. 9).

Many economists still agree with this answer. Indeed, it is enshrined as the conventional wisdom in many excellent textbooks (Ellsworth, 1964, p. 360; Kindleberger, 1963, pp. 506–8). But it is fallacious wisdom, as Fritz Machlup has correctly pointed out in another important essay (Machlup, 1958). To insist that there are no new restrictions is to make a value judgement: equality of supply and demand of foreign exchange in the absence of new restrictions is good, equality in their presence is bad. Value judgements are necessary in politics and in policy making. In problems of analysis, however, they simply confuse the issue. It is one thing to employ equilibrium analysis as a means of maximizing certain moral values or political goals; it is quite another thing to incorporate these values or goals into the definition of equilibrium itself. An evaluative equilibrium concept lacks much analytical usefulness. 'By infusing a value judgement, a political philosophy or programme, or a rejection of a programme or policy, into the concept of equilibrium designed for economic analysis, the analyst commits the fallacy of implicit evaluation or disguised politics' (Machlup, 1958, p. 124).

Like all fallacies, the fallacy of disguised politics ought to be avoided. Accordingly, the definition of international equilibrium ought not to be encumbered with a constraint that the rate of exchange be compatible with some unique level of restrictions. Quite the opposite, it is more appropriate to define the equilibrium exchange rate *exclusive* of the level of restrictions. Conceived analytically, equilibrium in international payments is compatible with *any* level of restrictions.

The second possibly relevant variable is the level of employment. Nurkse argued that 'it is hardly proper to call the exchange rate a true equilibrium rate if it can be maintained only by means of depression and unemployment at home' (Nurkse, 1945, p. 10). And again the textbooks concur (Ellsworth, 1964, p. 360; Kindleberger, 1963, pp. 508–9). But this too implies a value judgement – more disguised politics – and so by the same reasoning also ought to be avoided. An equilibrium exchange rate should be defined independently of the level of employment. Conceived analytically, equilibrium in international payments is compatible with any level of employment (or rate of price inflation).[6]

6. Alternatively, we can say that there is a *different* equilibrium exchange rate compatible with *each* level of employment (or rate of price inflation), as well as with each level of restrictions. This is also what is meant by the relativity of equilibrium, as Joan Robinson has written: 'It is now obvious that there is no one rate of exchange which is the equilibrium rate corresponding to a given state of world demands and techniques. In any given situation there is an equilibrium rate corresponding to each rate of interest and level of effective demand, and any

Adjustment revisited

Thus, sufficiently defined, an equilibrium exchange rate is one that over the course of a period not longer than a year equates the demand and supply of foreign exchange. Neither the presence of full employment and price stability nor the absence of new restrictions is an integral part of the concept of international equilibrium. This is the moral of Machlup's (1958) essay. It means that from the point of view of balance-of-payments policy, there are really no grounds at all for restricting the range of 'legitimate' adjustments to the two classical mechanisms. All adjustments – so-called compensatory corrections as well as the classical mechanisms – are interchangeable in so far as the balance of payments is concerned. They are all roughly equivalent as means for reconciling differences between the demand and supply of foreign exchange at a given exchange rate.

Why then did Machlup's (1965a) essay argue that compensatory corrections are incapable of 'full equilibration', and why do many economists agree? Machlup offered two reasons for his point of view. Both are representative lines of argument; neither is very convincing. In the first place, Machlup suggests, compensatory corrections 'more often than not, have repercussions that frustrate the attempts', either because they produce unintended side-effects and circumventions, or because they invite competitive reactions on the part of other governments (p. 211). Now, this may be so, but duration of impact or probability of retaliation are hardly adequate grounds for distinguishing among adjustment policies. In the real world, the same is true of the clas-

---

rate of exchange, within very wide limits, can be turned into the equilibrium rate by altering the rate of interest appropriately. Moreover, any rate of exchange can be made compatible with any rate of interest provided that money wages can be sufficiently altered. The notion of *the* equilibrium exchange rate is a chimera. The rate of exchange, the rate of interest, the level of effective demand and the level of money wages react upon each other like the balls in Marshall's bowl, and no one is determined unless all the rest are given' (Robinson, 1947, p. 103).

sical adjustment methods, too. The corrective impact of deflation or devaluation, for instance, may also be relatively brief, and the risk of retaliation to either policy is in fact, quite high.

In the second place, Machlup suggests, compensatory corrections 'are injurious to efficiency in the allocation of productive resources' (p. 212). This is not necessarily the case. Tibor Scitovsky has pointed out the relevance of the general theory of the 'second-best' in this connexion:

... in a world in which the flow of a large segment of international transactions is slowed by import duties and quantitative restrictions, it is by no means certain that the imposition of similar restraints also on the remaining segment would lower the efficiency of resource allocation (Scitovsky, 1966a, pp. 198–9).

Indeed, allocative efficiency might even be *improved*. But even if it is *not* improved, there are hardly adequate grounds here, either, for distinguishing among adjustment policies. In the real world, the cost of restrictions in terms of output foregone actually tends to be quite small – in fact, often smaller than the cost of a deflation resulting in a modest increase of unemployment. At times, compensatory corrections may be the most efficient means of adjustment (Cooper, 1968, pp. 249–55).

Among adjustment policies, therefore, compensatory corrections must be regarded as no less 'legitimate' than the two classical mechanisms. The Machlup (1965a) essay is in error. Indeed, by referring to allocative efficiency, Machlup in 1965 appeared to imply a value judgement: equilibrium is defined inclusive of, not exclusive of, the level of restrictions. This is disguised politics. Machlup in 1958 would have disapproved of this.

International equilibrium is not the only objective of macro-economic policy. Governments aim as well at domestic equilibrium – that is, at full employment with price stability. At another level, their goal is general equilibrium: simultaneous international and domestic equilibrium. Regrettably, although the objectives of international and domestic equilibrium are related, they usually tend to be in conflict. This fact is basic to the theory of balance-of-payments policy. Occasions do arise, of course, when the two goals are entirely consistent in the sense that both can be attained jointly using just a single policy variable. In a situation of simultaneous payments deficit and demand inflation, for instance, demand deflation alone will sometimes suffice to realize both goals. Similarly, in a situation of simultaneous payments surplus and unemployment, demand inflation alone might be sufficient. And in situations of simultaneous

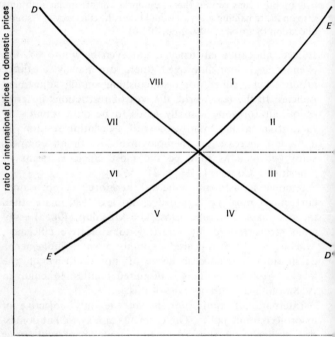

Figure 1 International equilibrium and domestic equilibrium determined by domestic real demand and the international price ratio

deficit and unemployment or of simultaneous surplus and inflation, currency devaluation or currency revaluation, respectively, alone might be effective. But these would be special cases. More generally, one policy variable will not be enough to attain jointly both policy objectives.

To understand why, consider Figure 1.[7] On the vertical axis is the ratio of international prices to domestic prices. This is an index of the country's foreign competitive position: the higher one moves up the scale, the larger are exports and the smaller are imports. On the horizontal axis is domestic real demand, which increases from left to right. The two curves shown in the figure represent, respectively, international equilibrium (EE') and domestic equilibrium (DD'). Both are drawn on the assumption that the price elasticities of domestic and foreign demand for imports together are sufficiently high (sum greater than unity) to ensure stability in the foreign-exchange market. The EE' curve is therefore shown with a positive slope, indicating that the more unfavourable the international price ratio becomes, the lower domestic real demand must be to maintain equilibrium of the balance of payments. Positions to the left and above the curve represent payments surplus; to the right and below, deficit. By analogous reasoning, the DD' curve is shown with a negative slope: the more unfavourable the international price ratio becomes, the higher domestic real demand must be to maintain full employment. Positions to the right and above the curve represent price inflation; to the left and below, unemployment.

Where the EE' and DD' curves intersect, the country is in general equilibrium. All other positions represent disequilibrium. However, from only a few of these disequilibrium positions can the country jointly attain the two policy objectives of international and domestic equilibrium by using just a single policy variable – specifically, from only those positions located on the horizontal and vertical dotted lines drawn through the intersection. In situations described

7. Figure 1 is adapted from a diagram first worked out by Trevor Swan (Swan, 1963, pp. 384–95).

by the horizontal line to the right, for instance, the ratio of international to domestic prices is appropriate, but domestic real demand is too high. Demand deflation alone would therefore suffice to realize both goals. Similarly, in situations described by the horizontal line to the left, demand is too low; demand inflation alone would be sufficient. And in situations described by the vertical line below or above the intersection, where demand is just right but the international price ratio is inappropriate, currency devaluation or currency revaluation, respectively, alone might be effective. But these are the special cases. In all other situations, both domestic demand and the international price ratio are inappropriate. As a result, the two policy objectives are in conflict, and the separate policy variables must be combined to be effective. In zones I and II, for instance, varying combinations of demand deflation and currency revaluation are required! and in zones III and IV, varying combinations of demand deflation and currency devaluation. In zones V and VI, varying combinations of demand inflation and currency devaluation are required; and in zones VII and VIII, varying combinations of demand inflation and currency revaluation.

These are specific instances of the more general problem with which the Dutch economist Jan Tinbergen was concerned: how to achieve a number of independent policy targets with a variety of effective policy instruments (Tinbergen, 1952). Tinbergen made the important observation that the number of instruments must not be smaller than the number of targets. In our context this means that the authorities responsible for international and domestic equilibrium must in general make use of at least *two* policy variables at all times.

This formulation follows the lead of James Meade's path-breaking treatise on *The Balance of Payments* (Meade, 1951, chapter 10). The core of Meade's analysis is a policy model consisting of two policy objectives and two policy variables. The objectives of policy are taken to be 'internal balance' and 'external balance'. The former is concerned with domestic incomes and prices, and is identical with a condition of full employment and price stability. The latter, by contrast, deals strictly with the balance of payments and, consistent with our own definition, is identical with a condition of equality of demand and supply of foreign exchange.[8] In a parallel manner, the two policy variables are taken to be income adjustments and price adjustments. Income adjustments operate through financial policy, price adjustments through exchange-rate variations or wage flexibility. The great achievement of Meade's book lies in the identification of these two policy variables and in the consequent integration of income and price effects. But herein lies a significant failure of the book as well; Meade falls prey to the fallacy of disguised politics (cf. Machlup, 1958, pp. 128–32). *General* price adjustments, and notably flexible exchange rates, are admitted as a policy variable, but not selective price adjustments operating through tariffs, subsidies, quotas, and other types of restrictions or controls. A value judgement is clearly implied. International equilibrium (external balance) is being defined inclusive of, not exclusive of, the level of restrictions. This we now know to be inappropriate.

A preferable approach is to generalize Meade's model along the lines suggested in a famous essay by Harry Johnson (Johnson, 1961) which recalls that, *ex post*, the balance of payments equals the difference between real national income (output) and real national absorption (expenditures):

$$B = Y - A,$$

where B represents the balance of payments, Y domestic income, and A domestic absorption (see chapter 1). If payments are in deficit, domestic expenditures exceeding out-

8. Following the example of Meade and virtually all other theorists, we shall in the discussion that follows assume that 'external balance' is in fact a desirable policy objective, and that it does in fact motivate the makers of balance-of-payments policy. This is a convenient assumption. See, however, the final section of this chapter, and also chapter 4.

put, the authorities must either reduce expenditures (A) or increase output (Y). To reduce expenditures they can operate directly by way of financial policy. On the other hand, to increase output they must operate indirectly by influencing the demand for production: spending (by residents or foreigners) on domestic output must be expanded; but spending must be expanded without adding to the total level of domestic expenditures (A), for this would nullify any increases of output (Y). Given the total level of spending, this in turn means that some part of the sum of domestic and foreign expenditures must be *switched* from foreign output to domestic output. It should be clear that depending on the circumstances, this may be accomplished as readily by selective price adjustments as by the general price adjustments admitted by Meade.

In other words, the authorities may make use of two types of policy variable: *expenditure-reducing or increasing policies* (financial policies) and *expenditure-switching policies* (exchange-rate variations, trade restrictions, capital restrictions,[9] exchange controls). This is the most general statement possible of the range of instruments available for dealing with problems of payments imbalance. At the same time the authorities are concerned with two policy objectives: internal balance and external balance. Our problem now is to consider some of the more important factors influencing the government's choice among these various policies.

9. Capital restrictions are included because capital movements, like current-account transactions, can be subjected to selective price adjustments operating through tariffs, subsidies, quotas, etc. They can also be influenced by monetary policy operating on the level of domestic expenditure and asset holding. It seems symmetrical to group the former with expenditure-switching policies and the latter with expenditure-reducing or increasing policies. In effect, real national absorption (A) is redefined to include not just domestic expenditures ($C + I + G$), but also expenditures for net *autonomous* capital exports.

Factors Influencing the Choice

Among the most important of the many factors are the relative impact of each instrument on each target; the source of the disturbance to the balance of payments; the extent of international consultation and co-operation; the distribution of the costs of adjustment; and conflict among the external policy objectives of the separate national governments.

Relative impacts of instruments

In the first instance, the choice among the various payments policies should be based upon an analysis of their costs and benefits, so that a combination can be selected that will minimize the net costs of adjustment in terms of other variables such as unemployment, inflation, allocative efficiency, the distribution of income, the terms of trade and economic growth. As a rule, dynamic systems tend to be most stable – that is, the approach to equilibrium tends to be most direct – when individual variables respond to the separate markets on which they have a (relatively) dominant influence. It follows that the net costs of balance-of-payments adjustment will be minimized if each policy variable is paired with the objective on which it has the greatest relative impact. Robert Mundell calls this the 'principle of effective market classification'[10] (Mundell, 1960, pp. 169–70). He notes correctly, that the 'comparative advantages' of different payments instruments vary considerably with respect to alternative targets. Application of the principle of effective market classification reduces the unfavourable side effects of policies and hence minimizes the magnitude of the

10. The principle of effective market classification (Mundell has also referred to this as the 'assignment problem') is a necessary companion to Tinbergen's principle that the number of instruments must not be smaller than the number of targets. Tinbergen was concerned with the *existence* of a solution to the system. He did not assert that any given set of policy responses will in fact lead to that solution. To assert this, it is necessary to investigate the stability properties of a dynamic system. That is where Mundell's principle is applicable.

adjustments that must be made. If the principle is not observed, in practice a tendency may develop either for a cyclical approach to equilibrium or for instability.

In *The Balance of Payments* Professor Meade seemed to be aware of this principle, as he almost invariably tied each policy variable implicitly to a specific objective in manipulating his policy model. Usually financial policies were assigned to maintain internal balance, and exchange-rate variations to maintain external balance (Meade, 1951). For this procedure he was criticized by a number of economists, most notably by Ragnar Nurkse, who pointed out that each instrument affects *both* the internal *and* the external situation. Expenditure policies, for instance, may also have incidental switching effects, to the extent that they influence the relative structure of prices as well as their absolute level. In the same way, switching policies may well have incidental expenditure effects: devaluation can alter the level of income through its impact on the balance of trade, and restrictions and exchange controls through their impact on allocative efficiency. Therefore, Nurkse insisted, it is purely arbitrary to associate one policy specifically with one aim and the other policy with the other aim (Nurkse, 1956).

However, in fact it is this criticism, not the procedure criticized, that is arbitrary. Of course it is true that each instrument affects both targets. But it is also true that the *relative* impact of each instrument on each of the two targets tends to be different. It matters considerably whether a policy variable is associated specifically with one aim or with another. Consider, for example, the imaginary country Cohenia, experiencing simultaneously unemployment at home and a deficit in its international transactions, and assume that the Cohenian authorities are prepared to make use of both their monetary and fiscal policies and a change of the exchange rate. Financial policies tend to have a relatively greater influence on the internal situation, exchange-rate changes a relatively greater influence on the external situation. Suppose, however, that the two instruments are paired incorrectly. Deflationary financial policy sufficient to achieve external balance would undoubtedly aggravate the domestic unemployment problem in Cohenia, and hence call for a quite sizeable devaluation of the national currency. A devaluation sufficient to achieve internal balance, though, would undoubtedly generate a surplus in the balance of payments, and hence call for a quite sizeable dose of *inflationary* financial policy, which in turn would call for a revaluation of the national currency, and so on. The situation would be markedly unstable. It is not inconceivable that internal and external balance might be attained jointly under these conditions, but it is probable that the approach to over-all equilibrium would be cyclical and unsteady. A steadier approach could be assured by tying each of the two policy variables directly to the objective on which it has the relatively greater impact.

In general, financial policies tend to have a relatively greater impact domestically, since *ex hypothesi* they operate directly on the level of expenditures and only indirectly on the balance of payments. Conversely, switching policies tend to have a relatively greater impact externally, since their most direct effect is on the volume and direction of international transactions. Thus governments are well advised to pair the former with the objective of internal balance and the latter with the objective of external balance.

Regrettably, governments do not always do what is best but rather what seems politically most practical. And the fact is that they do not always find it practical to make use of any of the alternative switching policies that are available to them – whether general price changes, exchange-rate changes, trade or capital restrictions, or exchange controls. Quite the opposite, as a matter of fact: owing to various political and legal considerations, governments often find it most expedient to avoid the use of all switching policies, and to rely instead solely on expenditure policies to achieve their objectives. The question is whether or not expenditure policies alone suffice to achieve the two objectives of internal and external balance. The answer, according to a 1962 article by Robert Mundell, is that they can, since there are also at least two types of expenditure policies – monetary policy and fiscal policy. It does not matter that the effects of the two types of financial policy on the two government objectives both tend to work in the same direction (e.g. both a rise of interest rates and a higher budget surplus lower demand for home goods and improve the balance of payments); it only matters that the effects of the two policies tend not to be identical. This makes them sufficient to attain the two policy targets. All that is needed, Mundell argues, is a judicious fiscal and monetary-policy 'mix' (Mundell, 1962).

Mundell's case for the mix is quite straightforward. It derives essentially from the differential impact of the two types of expenditure policies on the capital account of the balance of payments. For a given expenditure reduction, monetary policy and fiscal policy have the same effect on the trade account. However, in addition a rise of interest rates encourages inflows of foreign funds and so improves the capital account as well. It is manifest, therefore, that monetary policy has a relatively greater effect on the external situation than fiscal policy, and can be paired with the objective of external balance. Fiscal policy, meanwhile, can be paired with the objective of internal balance. It will then be possible to attain the two policy targets jointly. For instance, consider the example of Cohenia, experiencing simultaneously unemployment at home and a deficit in international transactions. A substantial budget deficit combined with a significant rise of interest rates can raise the level of domestic expenditures on balance, while at the same time attracting an inflow of capital from abroad. If the adjustment is right, both internal and external balance can be effectively achieved.

The case for the mixing is demonstrated by Figure 2, in which external balance (EE') and internal balance (DD') are plotted against the government budget surplus and the interest rate, representing (respectively) fiscal policy and

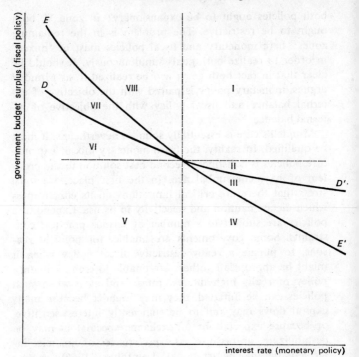

Figure 2 External and internal balance determined by monetary and fiscal policy

monetary policy.[11] Both curves are drawn with negative slopes, owing to the tendency of the two types of financial policy to work in the same direction. However, the slope of the EE' curve is made steeper to indicate the relatively greater impact of monetary policy on the external situation, internal balance being more responsive to fiscal policy. In zones I and V, there is no inconsistency in jointly using monetary and fiscal policy as one instrument: in zone I,

11. The EE' and DD' curves are the same as in Figure 1, drawn for a given ratio of international prices to domestic prices. Figure 2 is adapted from Mundell (1962).

both policies ought to be expansionary; in zone V, both ought to be restrictive. The problem is in the remaining zones: here monetary and fiscal policies must be 'mixed' in order to realize both goals simultaneously. It should be clear that in fact both goals *will* be realized if, as Mundell argues, monetary policy is paired with the objective of external balance and fiscal policy with the objective of internal balance.[12]

Mundell's case is essentially sound – nevertheless, it must be qualified. In reality, the fiscal-monetary mix of expenditure policies is a distinctly second-best solution to the problem of payments imbalance. In the first place, we must stress that there are critical limitations on its effectiveness which dictate caution and selectivity in its use. Expenditure policies are subject to a number of serious practical constraints. Some governments are unable, for political reasons, to pursue a really restrictive fiscal policy when it might be appropriate, others are unable to embark upon a policy of really high interest rates. And even when such policies can be initiated, they may founder because many capital flows may fail to be sufficiently interest-sensitive, or because expectations of exchange speculators may be destabilizing, or because asset preferences of financial intermediaries may be 'irrational' (Lamfalussy, 1966).

In addition, we must stress that the possibility of conflicts between the mixes of separate governments is considerable. As Harry Johnson has written:

12. Zone VII, for instance, corresponds to the example of Cohenia in the text: a situation of simultaneous unemployment and payments deficit. Internal and external balance will be effectively achieved if interest rates are raised at the same time that fiscal policy is shifted to less budget surplus or more budget deficit. (The reverse combination of easier money together with tighter fiscal policy would generate a movement away from equilibrium toward the north-west.) Varying mixes of tighter money and easier fiscal policy are also called for in zones VI (although corresponding, like zone V, to a situation of simultaneous inflation and payments deficit) and VIII (although corresponding, like zone I, to a situation of simultaneous unemployment and payments surplus). Conversely, varying mixes of easier money and tighter fiscal policy are called for in zones II and IV as well as in zone III.

Arriving at the right combination of fiscal and monetary policies in all countries simultaneously, especially if the adjustment of policies takes place by sequential trial and error, will be a complicated process and may in some circumstances lead away from rather than towards equilibrium (Johnson, 1966).

Finally, we must stress that fundamentally the fiscal-monetary mix is not really a true adjustment mechanism at all; at best it is just a palliative. It does not *adjust* the balance of payments, it merely *stabilizes* it. Flows of funds simply fill the gap between autonomous demand and supply of foreign exchange, leaving prices and incomes unchanged. In effect, the mix is no different from elementary financing of an imbalance, or from official intervention in the forward-exchange market. It will still be necessary to generate a marginal reallocation of resources in order to correct the initial disequilibrium situation and permit fiscal and monetary policy to revert to being directed by domestic rather than external considerations. And this will require either incomplete application of the indicated policy mix, or else its supplementation by additional policy measures of a switching type (Johnson, 1966).[13]

The supplementary switching policy most often recommended in this context is an 'incomes policy' – that is, a set of more or less rigidly enforced guideposts intended to hold down wage and price increases in deficit countries relative to those in surplus countries. Ideally, over time this should produce a general price adjustment sufficient to correct the initial imbalance: foreign and domestic expenditures will be switched from foreign output to domestic

13. These cautionary remarks apply even more strongly to attempts to 'mix' the components of just one type of financial policy – say, monetary policy. In the early 1960s the United States inaugurated 'Operation Twist', which was an attempt to use monetary policy alone to achieve both internal and external balance. High short-term rates were supposed to attract inflows of interest-sensitive international capital, thus reducing the balance-of-payments deficit, while low long-term rates were supposed to encourage a faster rate of growth at home. Needless to say, the effort to 'twist' the interest-rate structure met with only limited success. See chapter 4.

output. Unfortunately, in practice matters do not always work out so favourably, mainly because incomes policies tend to be rather slow-working, whereas pressures for adjustment may be quite immediate. Incomes policies also have additional limitations (Niehans, 1966). This emphasizes the need for correct diagnosis – for fitting the choice of adjustment policies to the requirements of the disequilibrium situation. And this in turn implies a need to identify the sources of disturbances. 'The appropriate speed of adjustment . . . depends on the cause of the maladjustment' (Harrod, 1966, p. 137).

Sources of disturbances

There is widespread agreement among economists that the choice of payments policies should be tailored to the nature of the disequilibrium. Edward Bernstein has written: 'The remedies for balance-of-payments difficulties should be selected in the light of their causes' (Bernstein, 1956, p. 159). And Fritz Machlup has written: 'To locate the source of a disturbance that has led to an imbalance of payments may be important for decisions about the most appropriate remedial measures' (Machlup, 1966a, p. 40). Even most government officials concur in this general approach to the adjustment problem. In August 1966 the Organization for Economic Cooperation and Development (O.E.C.D.) issued a *Report*, prepared by its Working Party No. 3, on *The Balance of Payments Adjustment Process* (O.E.C.D., 1966).[14] The primary emphasis of the

14. The O.E.C.D. comprises all of the countries of Western Europe, Canada, Japan, and the United States. Working Party No. 3 consists of treasury and central-bank officials representing Canada, France, Germany, Italy, Japan, the Netherlands, Sweden, Switzerland, the United Kingdom and the United States. The *Report* was written at the invitation of the Ministers of Finance of the Group of Ten (the same group of countries, with the exception of Belgium in place of Switzerland; the latter meets with the Group of Ten only on an *ex officio* basis), and was intended to be complementary to the studies then being made in the Group of Ten concerning international liquidity and monetary reform. A collection of essays was prepared for a preliminary meeting of academic economists with Working Party No. 3 (Fellner *et al.*, 1966).

Report was on means of improving the adjustment process, with one entire section devoted to an exhaustive taxonomy of 'Prescriptions for General Economic Policy' (paragraphs 41–51). Without exception, these prescriptions relate individual adjustment policies directly to specific causes of imbalance.

This does not mean that imbalances can be adjusted only by *treating* their causes. That is not the point. The point simply is that balance-of-payments policy, to be effective, must *take account* of causes.[15] Sometimes it is the causes of imbalances that must be treated, sometimes it is rather their symptoms or their consequences. It all depends on the circumstances.

What are the specific causes of imbalances? To begin with, we may characterize disturbances by their duration. Suppose a country experiences a sudden outflow of capital causing a deficit in its external transactions. The disturbance may be regarded as *reversible* if it is expected that there will be an inflow of approximately the same amount before the end of the relevant time period; as *temporary* if neither an inflow nor a further outflow is expected; as *continuing* if approximately the same outflow is expected; and as *progressive* if an even larger outflow is expected (Machlup, 1966a, p. 42).[16]

Disturbances that can be clearly identified as reversible pose the fewest problems for policy makers. Being the product of regular variations of output or prices, they tend by definition to correct themselves over a period of a week, a month, or at most a year. An outflow now is matched by

15. This elementary point does not seem to have been clear to Gottfried Haberler, who consequently argued in a recent essay that 'only in rare cases can or should the cure of a deficit be tailored to the nature of the cause' (Haberler, 1966, p. 126).

16. Disturbances can of course cause surpluses as well as deficits. However, for ease of exposition this paragraph and those that follow concentrate exclusively on the policy implications of negative disturbances (deficits). The policy implications of positive disturbances (surpluses), in each case being the converse of what appear in the text, are left to the ingenuity of the reader.

an inflow later. Thus the only need is to finance the imbalance for its duration. Generally the private market can be relied upon to accomplish this financing on its own. However, if stabilizing speculative or arbitrage flows happen to be insufficient for this purpose, the authorities themselves can sell foreign exchange, in the full expectation of replenishing their reserves when the imbalance is reversed. The only trouble arises if official reserves (and external credit facilities) also happen to be inadequate, as is sometimes the case with, say, less developed agricultural-exporting countries. In that event, some kind of switching policy will be necessary, preferably a selective policy – trade or capital restrictions or exchange controls – that can be easily discarded when the disturbance rights itself.[17] Expenditure policy, meanwhile, can be employed to maintain internal balance.

Temporary disturbances are a bit more difficult to deal with than reversible disturbances, principally because in this type of contingency the authorities cannot anticipate replenishing their reserves automatically over time. The imbalance will end of its own accord, but by definition it will not reverse itself. Temporary disturbances originate in some random event in the domestic economy or elsewhere – e.g. a crop failure or bumper harvest, a strike, a war or civil strife. For the duration of the event stabilizing flows of funds will be needed, but when the event is ended further flows are unlikely, except by chance. For that reason

17. Devaluation would be inappropriate under these conditions because trade or capital movements need to be restricted only temporarily, not irreversibly. That choice is ruled out. But another choice must be made – as between taxes (tariffs, surcharges, etc.), quantitative restrictions (quotas), or exchange controls. Quotas and exchange controls suspend the price system, introducing a wholly arbitrary new dimension into the international system. Taxes would therefore be preferable if the demand and supply of goods or funds were sufficiently elastic. But in fact short-run elasticities tend to be rather low, implying that the magnitude of a tax required to provide a given measure of relief may be extremely large. Hence taxes are usually a poor device to give temporary protection: the effects of quotas or exchange controls are much more certain.

financing by the private market is less certain, financing by
the authorities correspondingly more essential. No trouble
arises if official reserves (and external credit facilities) are
adequate for the purpose of once-over financing. However
if they are not adequate, once again some kind of switching policy will be called for. Whether it should be a selective policy or a general devaluation cannot be determined
a priori but must be decided in light of the circumstances
of the particular case.[18]

The most difficult problems for policymakers are posed
by continuing and progressive disturbances, which not only
do not reverse themselves automatically, but also do not
even tend to end of their own accord. Consequently, the
authorities are obliged to respond with genuine adjustment
policies, even if for a time official reserves seem adequate;
eventually they will surely become inadequate, unless in
the meantime some marginal reallocation of resources is
promoted to re-establish an equilibrium rate of exchange.
What kind of resource reallocation would be most appropriate depends on the source of the disturbance.

Continuing and progressive imbalances may be caused
either by 'monetary' disturbances or by 'structural' disturbances. There are two varieties of monetary disturbance. The first, called 'current inflation'[19] by Bernstein, is
manifested by excessive spending – that is, by a level of
real domestic absorption in excess of the value of available
output at constant prices (Bernstein, 1956, pp. 152–4).
The most common reason for current demand inflation is
excessive credit expansion. The most appropriate response,
therefore, is disinflationary financial policy. Devaluation
or some other switching policy would be self-defeating
so long as the level of internal demand continues to be

18. For example, how high is the country's average tariff rate? If it
is below the optimum tariff rate for that country, then the authorities
should restrict trade additionally rather than devalue; but if the average
rate is above the optimal rate, devaluation would be preferable. See
Alexander (1951).

19. The O.E.C.D. *Report* (1966) prefers the label 'inappropriate
level of internal demand'.

inappropriate. Only a genuine expenditure-reducing policy can fully adjust the balance of payments. We may note that in this special instance (assuming general equilibrium initially) one policy instrument happens to be enough to achieve both policy objectives – internal balance as well as external balance.

The second variety of monetary disturbance, called 'price and cost disparity'[20] by Bernstein, reflects an inflated level of home prices and costs (Bernstein, 1956, pp. 154, 155). Frequently, current demand inflation, especially in its early stages, has little impact on the structure of domestic production costs because the balance of payments tends to act as a safety valve. Sooner or later, however, an excessive level of expenditures is certain to bring about a substantial rise of wages and prices. As a result, exporters and producers of import-competing products will find their competitive position impaired, even after the demand inflation itself is halted. In this instance one policy instrument would not be enough to achieve both policy objectives. Expenditure-reducing policies alone might be effective in removing the external deficit, but only at the expense of employment, since prices and wages tend generally to be downwardly rigid. In the same way, expenditure-switching policies alone would almost certainly upset internal balance. This is the more general situation: a combination of both instruments must be administered, financial policies being assigned to maintain internal balance, while some kind of switching policy is employed to improve the country's international competitive position. If we assume that the price-cost disparity is generalized throughout the economy, we may conclude that the most appropriate switching policy would also be the most general one – namely, devaluation.

Structural disturbances come from changes in economic variables which, because they are not amenable to official manipulation in the short run, are usually treated analytically as parameters. Part of the dynamics of a growing

20. The O.E.C.D. *Report* (1966) prefers the label 'inappropriate international competitive position'.

world economy, such changes generally take the form of shifts in the demand and supply schedules of a country's exports and imports, or of variations in the rate of international capital flows (which may or may not be a function of changes in 'real' demand and supply conditions) (Bernstein, 1956, pp. 155–7).[21] To the extent that structural disturbances lead to a deterioration of the country's real international economic position – its needs for foreign exchange or its capacity to earn foreign exchange – some combination of the two types of adjustment policy will be called for. Again, expenditure policies will be most suitably employed to maintain internal balance, while some kind of switching policy is tied to the objective of external balance. However, unless the structural changes are widespread, devaluation in these circumstances may well be inappropriate. A much more effective approach might be to direct certain selective policies specifically towards those industries or sectors in which the structural changes have occurred, or else towards those industries or sectors in which offsetting structural changes may be anticipated. Alternatively, if reserves are adequate, it might be possible to rely exclusively on an incomes policy to bring about the desired switches of foreign and domestic expenditures.

This last possibility underscores a point rightly stressed by Peter Kenen, that 'financing and adjustment should be considered as complements rather than rivals', at least in so far as continuing and progressive disturbances are concerned (Harrod, 1966; Kenen, 1966, p. 152). In so far as reversible or temporary disturbances are concerned, of course, financing is a substitute for adjustment: it permits the authorities to avoid unnecessary or undesired reallocations of resources. But, *ex hypothesi*, when the disturbance is monetary or structural, resources must be reallocated. How resources will be reallocated depends upon whether the authorities choose an adjustment policy that takes effect as rapidly as, say, disinflation, or one that takes

21. The O.E.C.D. *Report* (1966) recognizes only one kind of structural change – 'excessive inflows or outflows of capital'.

effect as slowly as, say, an incomes policy. It is clear from the foregoing discussion that occasions do arise when a slower-working adjustment policy would be preferred; a fast-working reaction to imbalance is not always the best reaction. But it should also be clear that it will be impossible for the authorities to opt for a slower policy if their reserves (and external credit facilities) appear to be inadequate to bridge the gap during which the adjustment process will be operating. The ability to finance thus limits the effective range of policy alternatives. Governments can choose from the full range of balance-of-payments policies only to the extent that sufficient international liquidity is available to them.[22]

It is manifest, therefore, that the actual choice of adjustment policies is a difficult matter. True, the prescriptions for policy just outlined are relatively clear and straightforward, and do provide useful guidelines by which balance-of-payments policy may be formulated. Even so, the task of the policy maker can hardly be described as a simple one. As the O.E.C.D. *Report* 1966, para. 48 warns :

The ... preceding paragraphs provide a set of presumptions concerning the appropriate broad types of measure which should at least form a useful framework within which adjustment policies can, in individual cases, be discussed and evaluated. But they can be regarded as no more than a highly simplified framework, since, as recent experience shows, imbalances are frequently of a far more complex nature.

The problem is one of *diagnosis*. In any given situation in the real world, it is quite difficult to identify empirically the precise source of a balance-of-payments disturbance. Is the imbalance temporary or continuing? Is its cause monetary or structural? The problem of diagnosis is com-

---

22. On the other hand, if sufficient liquidity is available to them, governments may not always use it to complement the most appropriate adjustment policy. On the contrary, they may use it as a substitute for adjustment of any kind. This suggests that the rate of creation of new liquidity should be discretionary, and should be aligned with the most desirable pace of adjustment in each country (Kenen, 1966).

plicated, moreover, by the fact that, often, a single disturbance has not one but multiple sources. Indeed, only rarely can an actual imbalance be attributed solely to just one cause. It is much more common to find several different factors each contributing to the disequilibrium in varying degrees. The questions must then be: what is the predominant cause? Can several instruments of policy be combined? The conclusion is that there are no simple answers. That way lies *naïveté*. Judgement is indispensable.[23]

International consultation

Judgement in the making of balance-of-payments policy is aided by international consultation and co-operation. Without consultation there is a considerable danger of conflict among national policies, both with respect to priorities among official *objectives* and with respect to the *instruments* chosen to achieve those objectives. In the first place, the over-all policy targets specified independently by different national governments may be inconsistent – if, for instance, all governments aim simultaneously to secure a secular rise of foreign-exchange reserves (see below, the section entitled 'Conflicts among external policy objectives'). It is impossible for all countries to earn surpluses at the same time. And in the second place, even if the over-all

23. It may be useful in this connexion to note that the problem of diagnosis and judgement lies at the heart of the fixed-versus-flexible-exchange-rate controversy. Advocates of flexible exchange rates believe it is hardly possible to diagnose correctly the various types of disturbances at a sufficiently early stage and that therefore irreversible mistakes will be made too often if the authorities attempt to determine on an *ad hoc* basis whether prolonged financing or prompt adjustment is appropriate. They contrast this danger of error with the (presumed) smoothness and easy reversiblity of adjustment with flexible rates.

The answer to this argument is simple. *Someone* must make the diagnosis, *either* the national authorities (under pegged rates) *or* private foreign-exchange dealers (under rate flexibility), and there is no assurance that the latter are necessarily more prescient than the former. Errors of judgement are possible under either system. The key question is this: under which system are such errors likely to be minimized? Unfortunately, this is an empirical question that cannot be answered *a priori*.

policy targets are not inconsistent, the desired compositions of the separate payments balances may be so – if, for instance, all governments aim simultaneously to secure a net surplus on current account sufficient to offset planned transfer transactions and outflows on capital account. This is impossible, too. Finally, assume all official targets happen to be compatible. Conflict among national policies is still possible, if the instruments chosen to achieve those targets are incompatible – if, for instance, some countries rely on expenditure policies to avoid payments imbalance while others rely on switching policies; or, alternatively, if all countries rely on the fiscal-monetary mix but some use monetary policy to maintain internal rather than external balance.

To the extent that there is any conflict among national policies, three consequences ensue. First, the instability of the system is increased. The government of any one country is likely to be confronted with larger and more frequent disturbances to the balance of payments than if all governments were agreed on targets and instruments. In addition, the process of adjustment is slowed down. Any one government is likely to discover that it takes longer to achieve internal or external policy objectives, since its own actions will often evoke policy reactions by others tending to weaken the influence of the measures initially instituted. And this in turn implies a third consequence – namely, that as such counteracting motions accumulate, all countries are likely to find themselves worse off than they need be. Each government will find that the process of policy competition is mutually damaging (Cooper, 1968, chapter 6).

Today, international consultation on balance-of-payments policy is carried out in a number of forums, including most notably the International Monetary Fund, the Bank for International Settlements (B.I.S.) and the O.E.C.D. The principal value of such consultation is that it can ensure a greater compatibility of national policy targets and instruments. In practice, it is possible to improve both diagnosis and therapy. By consulting, governments find they can more rapidly identify impending imbalances and also more accurately analyse the sources of disturbances and their probable duration. In addition, they can confer on the optimal timing of remedial measures and on the proper pace of adjustment. And they can review their over-all and compositional policy objectives, amending them wherever appropriate.[24] As a result, a much more efficient choice among the various balance-of-payments policy alternatives is possible. With compatibility of targets and instruments maximized, the costs of adjustment can be minimized.

The costs of adjustment cannot, however, be eliminated. International consultation is not a substitute for a re-allocation of resources at the margin. Consultation can minimize the size of the margin, by avoiding unnecessary conflict among national policies. But consultation cannot make the resource reallocation unnecessary (assuming the initial payments disturbance is continuing or progressive). Some adjustment must be made; the costs must be paid. The nations must still agree on who will sacrifice what – that is, they must agree on the distribution of the costs of adjustment between surplus and deficit countries.

Distribution of adjustment costs

It is useful to distinguish between two different costs inherent in the process of balance-of-payments adjustment, one a 'transitional' cost, one a 'continuing' cost (Cohen, 1966, pp. 3–11). The latter is never shared. The former, though, may be paid by either surplus or deficit countries. The distribution of the transitional cost of adjustment,

---

24. The O.E.C.D. *Report* (1966) specifically recommends an early warning system to facilitate early identification of emerging imbalances; reviews of short-term balance-of-payments forecasts; confrontations of national policies; and exchanges of information regarding national balance-of-payments aims. See paragraphs 65–71. See also chapters 2–4 (by Fellner, Machlup and Triffin) of *Maintaining and Restoring Balance in International Payments* (Fellner *et al.*, 1966), each of which is intended to help in formulating general principles of international consultation on diagnosis and therapy.

therefore, is an important factor in the choice among policy alternatives.

Real adjustment requires a country in deficit to decrease its imports of goods and services relative to its exports of goods and services – in other words, to decrease real national absorption relative to real national income (see above, the section entitled 'Adjustment revisited'). At the new international equilibrium, the former debtor must be worse off than its trading partners: it must now receive a smaller proportion of combined global output than before. This is the *continuing* cost of balance-of-payments adjustment. It is a continuing cost in that it is an open-ended phenomenon – the continuing real sacrifice that the new international situation, prevailing after all change has occurred, imposes on the former deficit country. *Ex hypothesi,* this cost is always borne entirely by the deficit country, whatever the particular method of adjustment used at the time.

In addition, the process of adjustment also imposes a *transitional* cost – the cost of the required reallocation of resources, which is separate and quite distinct from the presumed cost of the new situation obtaining after that re-allocation is complete. This sacrifice is the cost of change, and can be measured directly in terms of real national income foregone (unlike the continuing cost of adjustment, which is measured in terms of real national absorption foregone and can therefore be expressed only indirectly as a function of changes in real national income). Plainly, some part or even virtually all of the transitional cost of adjustment may be borne by either the deficit or the surplus country. True, the adjustment process itself must be shared; the required reallocation of resources must be complementary. But the cost of the resource reallocation may be paid for largely or even wholly by either debtor or creditor. With respect to the transitional cost of adjustment, there does exist a problem of international distribution.

What, in practice, is the distribution of the transitional

cost of adjustment? This is a problem of positive (descriptive) economics. The majority of economists seem to think that because of the pressure of reserve losses, most of the cost tends to be paid by the deficit country. In chapter 2 we noted that while there is virtually no limit to how much foreign exchange a government can accumulate, there is a definite limit to how much it can sell. This means that the compulsions to adjust tend to be asymmetrical: the deficit country must usually be the first to take corrective measures. From this it is commonly inferred that the deficit country must also pay the largest part of the cost of the correction (Scitovsky, 1965). This, however, is a false inference, for in fact there is no reason to assume that the country that pays the transitional cost of adjustment need be the same as the country that initiates the adjustment process, particularly if expenditure-switching policies are being relied upon to achieve external balance. Such policies are by definition substitutes for a direct realignment of internal money incomes and spending. As such, they can readily serve to transfer the transitional adjustment cost from the deficit country to others (Cohen, 1966, pp. 11–12). This had led a few economists to suggest that perhaps it is the surplus countries that must usually pay the largest part of the cost of adjustment, not the deficit countries as generally supposed. Certainly it is significant that in many instances surplus countries prefer to extend large and long-continued flows of credit to deficit countries rather than force the latter to adjust – in effect, bribing debtors not to devalue or impose exchange controls or other severe restrictions on trade and investment. Apparently, creditors are willing to do this because they have found that bribes are less expensive than genuine adjustment. As Herbert Stein (1965) has said, 'the potential lenders discovered that it was really in their interest to lend'.[25]

25. In my monograph I suggested that it is probably a mistake to concentrate exclusively on who is in deficit and who is in surplus in identifying the distribution of the transitional cost of adjustment. I argued rather that the basic explanation is to be found in the economic

This raises a second problem, of normative (prescriptive) economics: what *should* be the distribution of the transitional cost of adjustment? This is the immediate question for the makers of balance-of-payments policy. We may distinguish two cosmopolitan criteria for establishing the respective obligations of surplus and deficit countries. In the first place, responsibilities might be allocated with reference to the sources of disturbances (Cohen, 1966, pp. 19–20). However, even apart from the problem of diagnosis, this criterion is relatively clear-cut only in certain situations – specifically, in situations of imbalance caused by monetary disturbances, when we may confidently assert that most or all of the cost ought to be paid by the country in which the disturbance originates. But what of imbalances caused by structural developments? In these situations a set rule based on causation cannot be so easily applied. Suppose a country suddenly experiences a payments deficit because of a shift of consumer tastes away from home goods in favour of imports. Should that country be expected to pay *all* of the adjustment cost, contracting demand until such time as the deficit is wholly eliminated? Should other nations be expected to pay *none*, refraining entirely from monetary expansion despite the net increase of demand for their products? Presumably, in a case such as this, all nations should be expected to share the cost together, though in what proportions it is impossible to say merely on the basis of causation. Similarly, all nations ought to share the adjustment cost required by other kinds of structural changes involving technology or factor endowments, though again the proportions are uncertain. The criterion of causation in these situations is inadequate as a guide to policy.

As a supplement to the criterion of causation in situations of structural disturbance, James Tobin has proposed that responsibilities be allocated with reference to the 'cir-

---

structure of nations (Cohen, 1966, pp. 22–9). A similar argument has been proposed by Robert Mundell (1968a, pp. 192–4).

cumstances' of each country relative to the economic objectives of all nations taken together (Tobin, 1966; see also Fleming, 1968, and Mundell, 1968a, chapter 13). Circumstances are defined by two variables, rates of unemployment and rates of price increase, with adjustment obligations being assigned in relation to them jointly. The aim is to stay as near as possible to the target of full employment without inflation for the world as a whole. It is implied that each country ought to share the transitional cost of adjustment more or less in proportion to its ability to contribute to that global target.

Unfortunately, few countries are likely to agree with these cosmopolitan criteria – or any others, for that matter. It is the fallacy of composition to assume that what is best for the world as a whole will also be seen as best by each country individually. In reality, governments aim at a different target. What they want is to stay as near as possible to full employment without inflation for themselves – consequently to minimize the costs of adjustment that they themselves must pay – irrespective of the sources of disturbances or the circumstances of the world economy. Governments choose their policies in the light of interests interpreted nationally, even when forums exist for consultation at the international level. And in so far as the choice of adjustment policies is concerned, the national interest is interpreted to mean the least possible sacrifice at home. From the perspective of the individual country, the 'best' distribution of the transitional adjustment cost is that distribution which obliges the other fellow to pay it all. The process of adjustment, therefore, tends in fact to be a matter of considerable power play, as the capacity of each country to avoid transitional costs is constantly matched against the corresponding capacity of every other country. This helps to explain why in practice the adjustment problem is so difficult to resolve. In its essence, it represent a fundamental clash of national interests (Cohen, 1966, pp. 20–21).

Conflicts among external policy objectives

The clash of national interests in the adjustment process manifests itself most clearly in the conflict among the external policy objectives of the separate national governments. Previously, following the example of most writers on the subject, we have assumed that the common objective of all payments policies is 'external balance'. Now it is time to relax that assumption. From the point of view of any one country or from the viewpoint of the world as a whole, equality of demand and supply of foreign exchange may not always be the most desirable goal of policy; it may instead be surplus or deficit.

The pure theory of exchange rates shows that from the point of view of any one country, balance-of-payments surpluses are not inherently desirable, since they imply a reduction of real domestic absorption relative to real national income. Conversely, deficits are not inherently undesirable, since they permit any one country to absorb more than its current income – in effect, to 'live beyond its means'. But for just that reason most economists are opposed to deficits as a desirable goal of policy. Tibor Scitovsky calls this the 'puritan ethic of international trade' (Scitovsky, 1966b, p. 1212). It asserts that from the viewpoint of the world as a whole, it is wrong for any one country to get 'something for nothing'. But is it wrong?

What is wrong with it, I think, is that it is ethics rather than economics. Not only is it perfectly good economics occasionally to get something for nothing; it is or should be one of the economist's main preoccupations. It is, indeed, the subject matter of welfare economics. To move from a non-optimal to a Pareto-optimum situation is the art of getting something for nothing (Scitovsky, 1966b, p. 1212).

This suggests that there may be times when balance-of-payments deficits are 'perfectly good economics' – when they may, in fact, serve to advance important cosmopolitan economic objectives. A case can be made, for instance. that the persistent payments deficits of the United States in the 1950s were probably desirable, because they provided a sustained and sound basis for the export-oriented post-war expansion of the Japanese and Western European economies (Cooper, 1964). In addition, though it seems less probable, a case can be made for claiming that these deficits remain desirable even today, because they provide the basis for a trade of liquidity (financial intermediation) between the United States and the rest of the world (Kindleberger, 1965a).[26] In the same way, a case can be made with respect to the less developed countries for saying that deficits would be desirable in the future, because they could alleviate the foreign-exchange bottleneck and thereby permit a more rapid rate of growth.

Despite these arguments, few countries actually do try to promote balance-of-payments deficits as an objective of policy. Once again, it is the fallacy of composition to assume that what is best for the world as a whole will also be seen as best by each country individually. From the point of view of each country individually, the best objective is usually surplus, despite the implied reduction of absorption relative to income. This is because of the tendency toward asymmetry in the compulsions to adjust under the Bretton Woods exchange system. It is true that in the adjustment process the country in deficit need not be the party that pays the cost of the correction. Nevertheless, the deficit country rather than the country in surplus must usually take the first corrective measures. In this sense, the surplus country exercises an important influence over the economy and policies of the deficit country. The influence may be implicit in the former country's accumulation of the latter country's reserves, or it may be made explicit in the form of conditions and 'strings' attached to the extension of credit facilities or balance-of-payments support. Either way, the situation represents for the deficit country a form of dependence that, in the light of its own national interest, it would prefer to avoid. The easiest way for a country to avoid such dependence is to add

26. See also chapter 4 (the discussion of the United States).

regularly to its reserves, thereby ensuring their continuing adequacy over time – to become a surplus country, capable of exercising an influence of its own. As the O.E.C.D. *Report* (1966, para. 17) acknowledges, 'it is clear that most countries wish to see a secular rise in their reserves. No country is prepared to have its reserves decrease over the longer run.'[27]

But it is clear, too, that not all countries can earn surpluses at the same time. Conflict among national policies is therefore inevitable.[28] International consultation may ease the conflict, and circumstances may alter its appearance, but the essential clash of national interests will not disappear. This emphasizes again why the adjustment problem is so difficult to resolve. The process of adjustment, by its nature, must be a matter of considerable power play, with the interplay of national power being expressed in the actual choices made of balance-of-payments policies. The problem for policy makers, as has been said, is to make the correct choices.

27. Fitz Machlup once explained the desire for secular reserve growth by analogy with his wife's wardrobe; this has since become known as the 'Mrs Machlup's Wardrobe Theory of Monetary Reserves' (Machlup, 1966b).

28. The danger of policy conflict is heightened by what Robert Mundell calls the 'redundancy problem'. Consider a world of n countries. If $n-1$ countries have balance-of-payments targets which they successfully achieve, the balance of payments of the nth country is automatically determined. It follows that unless at least one of the n countries in the system reacts passively to the policies of the others, a high probability of conflict arises (Mundell, 1968b).

4 Balance-of-Payments Policy: Practice

As the basic elements of the *theory* of balance-of-payments policy have now been surveyed, this chapter concludes with a discussion of some balance-of-payments policies in actual *practice*. We have seen in chapter 3 that the choice between policy alternatives is influenced by many factors. What we shall see in this chapter is how different countries actually do tend to respond to these factors in the event of serious payments imbalance.[1]

In this chapter the balance-of-payments responses of six major industrial countries are examined. The first section considers three instances of payments surplus: Canada in 1949–51, Germany in 1955–62 and France in 1959–64. The second section then considers three instances of payments deficit: Italy in 1962–5, the United Kingdom in 1964–7 and the United States in 1961–7. These examples have been selected because of their relatively recent origin, because of the importance of the countries involved, and because they effectively illustrate the several approaches that a country's financial authorities can – and do – follow in attempting to solve problems of payments imbalance. The purpose of this chapter will be to describe briefly and to compare; there is not enough space here for more detailed critical evaluation. The reader is advised to look beyond

---

1. Although payments imbalances are commonplace occurrences, only a few are serious enough to require more than merely a dose of financing or a marginal shift of past policies. Only a few, therefore, are useful for our illustrative purposes. This chapter, therefore, is highly selective: in order to bring out most clearly the *choice* among adjustment alternatives, all the examples discussed involve unusually serious disturbances.

these succinct introductions before making a final judgement regarding the appropriateness of the policy choices in each instance.

Balance-of-Payments Surpluses

When a country's balance of payments is in surplus, no intrinsic *external* constraint operates to compel the government to adjust. Indeed, if it chooses a government has the potential to finance a surplus indefinitely, simply by selling additional amounts of its own currency; foreign exchange can be accumulated virtually without limit. However, there *is* an intrinsic *internal* constraint operating to compel the government to adjust, a constraint which arises from the fundamental economic fact that when external receipts exceed payments, domestic purchasing power is expanded. In the short run, of course, the authorities can neutralize the inflationary impact of a surplus by means of simultaneously offsetting monetary and fiscal policies, but they cannot do so indefinitely. Domestic disinflation cannot be applied without limit, mainly because of political obstacles or institutional imperfections (Scott and Schmidt, 1964). If, therefore, the surplus persists for very long, demand and price inflation will almost inevitably ensue; and if the inflation is to be avoided, either the payments surplus must be eliminated or additional steps will be required to restrict domestic activity. This was the policy problem shared by Canada in 1949–51, Germany in 1955–62 and France in 1959–64.

Canada: 1949–51

Beginning in the last quarter of 1949 and continuing into 1950, Canada experienced a balance-of-payments surplus of unprecedented (for Canadians) magnitude. The immediate cause of the surplus was a flood of foreign, mainly United States, capital. The immediate result of the surplus was a rapid rise of official holdings of gold and U.S. dollars, particularly in the third quarter of 1950, when in one ten-week period alone $500 million was added to the reserves – nearly a 50 per cent increase. At first, the Canadian authorities sought merely to neutralize the domestic impact of the capital inflow, but the flood was just too great to handle. Financing, it became clear, would not be enough; some policy to adjust the balance of payments would be needed. The policy finally chosen was an expenditure-switching policy: exchange-rate variation (Wonnacott, 1965, chapter 3; Yeager, 1966, ch. 24).

The root cause of Canada's surplus in 1949–50 was the Government's decision to devalue the Canadian dollar by 10 per cent in September 1949, from parity with the U.S. dollar to a discount of 10 per cent. Behind that decision lay the exchange crisis of 1947–8, when the country had been in over-all deficit. The basic problem then was the inability of Canada's European trading partners to cover their current-account deficits *vis-à-vis* Canada with gold or convertible foreign exchange (i.e. U.S. dollars): in turn, this meant that Canada could not cover its traditional trade deficit *vis-à-vis* the United States. When in addition the usual inflow of American capital fell off early in 1947 and then became an outflow, Canadian reserves started to shrink drastically. Indeed, reserves would have been exhausted had the Government not begun in November 1947 to impose severe restrictions on trade, travel and foreign investments. The programme of exchange controls was sufficient to stem the crisis, but not to solve it. Inconvertible currencies earned in Europe still could not meet the continuing deficit with the United States. Thus pressure on the balance of payments persisted into 1949. Finally, when the worldwide devaluations of September of that year threatened Canada's exports with intensified competition, the authorities felt impelled to devalue the Canadian dollar as well.

People soon felt that the Canadian dollar was now undervalued and would surely have to be rapidly revalued. As a consequence, the balance of payments quickly swung into surplus. Trade movements played no appreciable role in the massive reserve accumulation after September 1949:

in fact, the total Canadian current-account balance was negative in each of the first three quarters of 1950. Capital movements were entirely responsible for the surplus. Moreover, these capital movements were for the most part speculative in nature. Of the roughly $1 billion of net capital imports in 1950, only about one-quarter was for the purpose of long-term investment. These consisted principally of direct capital expenditures by American corporations in oil, mining and manufacturing ventures. The main part of the inflow, three-quarters of the total, comprised short-term investments in Canadian bank deposits and securities, which grew at an increasing rate despite the fact that during the period in question yield differentials were actually shifting in favour of the United States. It is clear that these investments were sparked by the rumours of revaluation then sweeping Canada (Wonnacott, 1965, p. 78). They were motivated essentially by expectations of capital gain from an imminent appreciation of the Canadian dollar.

The Canadian authorities attempted initially to meet the speculative inflow by financing the surplus in the balance of payments. Thinking the capital imports would not last long, they decided it would be best just to try to *stabilize* the payments balance, not to *adjust* it. Consequently, they bought all the U.S. dollars offered in the foreign-exchange market. At the same time they sold Government securities on the open market at home, thus seeking to neutralize the inflationary effects of the inflow – in other words, to resist the private-market adjustment process. Relative to the size of the Canadian economy, these sales constituted the largest open market operation in the history of central banks to that time (Yeager, 1966, p. 424). Even so, they were insufficient to keep the domestic money supply from rising; the inflow was simply too big. By September 1950 it was quite obvious that unless the surplus was quickly ended, serious demand and price inflation in Canada would ensue. The authorities saw that they would have to eliminate the surplus directly via expenditure-switching policies. Otherwise it would be necessary to offset the surplus by disinflating the economy severely, and this was considered undesirable since the disturbance seemed likely to be reversible rather than continuing or progressive. Some type of switching policy was obviously needed.

Here diagnosis was crucial. The main source of the disturbance lay in the capital account; the current account, as we know, was in deficit, and in fact a further weakening of several strategic merchandise and service items seemed likely. Any relaxation of the trade and travel restrictions imposed in 1947–8, therefore, was immediately ruled out. The same decision applied to the possibility of relaxing any of the recent restrictions on Canadian investments abroad, since the available evidence indicated that liberalization would not significantly increase gross capital outflows (Wonnacott, 1965, p. 79). New controls might have been imposed directly on the flood of capital imports, but this course of action was rejected on the grounds that it might in the long run discourage the investments by foreigners that were so essential to the future growth of the Canadian economy. Thus, by process of elimination, official attention turned to the possibility of a change of the exchange rate.

Perhaps the simplest procedure might have been just to revalue the Canadian dollar to parity with that of the United States. However, three important considerations argued against establishing a higher *pegged* rate for the Canadian dollar. In the first place, a higher pegged rate would probably have reversed the short-term capital inflow since it would have given foreign speculators an attractive incentive to take their profits at the expense of the Canadian authorities. It is estimated that revaluation to par would have cost the Government some $67 million (Binhammer, 1964, p. 638). Secondly, as indicated, the current account was weakening. A higher pegged rate would have added to commercial difficulties that were already becoming apparent. And, finally, there was the problem of choosing an 'appropriate' pegged rate. The Canadian authorities had already tried and failed twice in the post-war period to locate an equilibrium exchange rate (prior to devaluing in 1949, they had revalued in 1946), and there was no assurance that they would be any more successful a third time. Consequently, they chose instead to abandon the Bretton Woods exchange system, and try a floating rate. The break with the I.M.F. régime – the only such instance involving a major country – was announced on 30 September 1950.

At the time, apparently, the break was supposed to be a temporary expedient, no more. Essentially, the Government's intention seems to have been to experiment with a free rate in the hope that it would eventually lead to an equilibrium rate which could then be pegged again in terms of other currencies. However, the immediate results of the new régime were better than had been anticipated by even the most sanguine of its advocates. Although the exchange rate for the Canadian dollar quickly moved up to a smaller discount *vis-à-vis* the U.S. dollar, American direct investments continued to move into Canada at a satisfactory pace. Meanwhile, the heavy speculative inflow of short-term capital ceased without giving rise to a speculative outflow, thus enabling the authorities progressively to abolish their general structure of exchange restrictions. By the time the last of these controls were abolished in December 1951, the Canadian balance of payments was healthier and more stable than ever in the post-war period. It is not surprising, therefore, that the Canadian Government decided at about this point to formalize the 'temporary' break with the I.M.F. system. Henceforth, it was the Government's intention, in effect, to rely upon the floating rate as a semi-automatic switching device to maintain external balance, with monetary and fiscal policies free to concentrate on the objective of internal balance. In fact, this combination of policies worked remarkably well in the ensuing years, until questionable management of financial policy – especially monetary policy – in 1958–61 finally forced a devaluation and pegging of the Canadian dollar in May 1962.[2]

Federal Republic of Germany: 1955–62

Although the West German balance of payments first emerged into surplus in 1951, it was not until 1955 that the Government of the Federal Republic began to take measures to control it. Earlier the surplus had been regarded by most observers as desirable, since Germany was thus enabled to acquire much-needed gold and dollars – reserve accumulation rather than external balance being at the time considered to be the proper objective of policy. But in 1955 sufficient concern was being aroused by the inflationary effects of the surplus on domestic demand and prices to impel the authorities to action. Soon their objective shifted to external balance rather than surplus. For the next half-decade the German Government tried out a variety of expenditure and switching policies in the hope of reconciling this goal with the complementary objective of internal balance. No truly decisive results were achieved, though, until finally the Deutsche mark (DM) was revalued by 5 per cent in March 1961 (Scammell, 1961, ch. 12; Yeager, 1966, ch. 23).

Germany's chronic surplus in the 1950s was the largest in the world. It reflected a sizeable and growing excess of merchandise exports over imports. Between 1950 and 1960, German exports rose at an average annual rate of 19 per cent. Since, however, imports increased only at an average rate of about 14 per cent, the trade surplus expanded almost without interruption. In most years, in fact, it actually exceeded the total surplus in the balance of payments (other transactions, on balance, being in deficit). What explains Germany's phenomenal competitive strength in

2. Since in this book the Bretton Woods system is taken to be the institutional framework of balance-of-payments policy, this chapter will not discuss the Canadian experience under flexible exchange rates. However, for discussions of this later experience see Binhammer, 1964; Johnson, 1964, pp. 25–7; Wonnacott, 1965, part II; Yeager, 1966.

world markets? There are many plausible explanations,[3] but no one of them tells the whole story. Hence they are probably best taken together. They suggest a continuing or progressive imbalance of multiple origins – an imbalance arising partly from changing structural factors inside the German economy, partly from a significant cost-price disparity between Germany and the rest of the world, and partly from a relatively greater degree of current inflation on the part of Germany's chief commercial rivals.

Manifestly, the choice of adjustment policies confronting Germany was a complex matter. The Government might, for instance, have chosen to accelerate the rate of demand and price inflation at home via expansionary financial policies. However, Germans have been obsessed by an almost pathological fear of rising prices ever since the hyperinflation that followed the First World War. In 1955–62, therefore, the authorities were extremely reluctant to inflate domestic demand as a means of reducing the foreign surplus. They preferred rather to rely on switching policies of various sorts, thus ensuring that financial policies could be directed toward the objective of maintaining internal balance.

The obvious switching policy to consider was of course the most general one – namely, a revaluation of the DM. This alternative appealed to logic, since everyone knew that the level of German prices had been rising more slowly than the price levels of most other industrial countries. Moreover, there was little doubt that the postwar parity of the DM, when settled in 1948, had reflected a considerable measure of deliberate under-valuation (Scammell, 1961, p. 367). But revaluation did not appeal to the German Government, mainly for political reasons: exporters would protest. So the authorities experimented with more selective switching policies instead. Early in the period they concentrated primarily on the current account, their intention being to redirect domestic demand so as

3. Charles Kindleberger cites more than a half dozen (Kindleberger, 1965b).

both to absorb some of the goods and services previously diverted to exports, and to increase imports. In 1956 they freed so-called dollar-area imports from quantitative restrictions to about the same extent as they had already done for intra-European trade; and they unilaterally reduced certain tariffs on manufactured imports. And in 1957 they completely eliminated the rationing of foreign exchange for travel abroad.

Regrettably, these measures were insufficient. The trade surplus continued to grow. So then the authorities shifted their attention to the capital account, hoping to be able to encourage capital exports and reduce capital imports. In 1958 full convertibility privileges were extended to residents of the Federal Republic as well as to non-residents, and the last remaining restrictions on German foreign investments were removed. And in 1960 various steps were taken to discourage capital inflows, such as the prohibition of interest on and the establishment of discriminatory reserve requirements for foreign deposits.

But these measures too were insufficient. Institutionally, Germany was not well equipped to be a capital exporter. On the contrary, the country was bound to be a capital importer so long as interest rates remained as high as they then were. High interest rates, however, were an essential part of the whole complex of financial policies then being employed to maintain internal balance. By the year 1960–61, therefore, the authorities found themselves caught on the horns of a classic dilemma. The foreign-trade surplus was bigger than ever. To avoid the inflationary implications of that surplus, a tight monetary policy was required. But a tight monetary policy was attracting additional foreign capital at an accelerating pace, thereby exacerbating the difficulties of neutralizing the domestic impact of the payments surplus. As in Canada in 1950 (though the circumstances were different), so in Germany in 1960–61, it was becoming increasingly clear that if a serious price inflation was to be avoided, the option of a change of the exchange rate would have to be reconsidered.

Germany does not seem to have thought seriously about the possibility of a floating exchange rate; no break with Bretton Woods was desired. Consequently, the authorities decided instead to peg the Deutsche mark at a new higher level, which became effective on 6 March 1961. At first, the smallness of the revaluation suggested possible repetition, and as a consequence hot money surged into the Federal Republic. But within a month the speculative flurry subsided, and within six months the effects of the revaluation were apparent in an easing of inflationary pressures and a shrinking of the trade surplus. Indeed, in 1962 the favourable trade balance was cut in half. Total payments were in deficit in both 1961 and 1962. In the years after 1962 the tendency toward persistent surplus in Germany's foreign balance reappeared. However, the tendency toward surplus was less powerful than before (and in financing the surplus the German authorities became much more sophisticated than before). The revaluation of the DM in 1961 may not have been great enough but it was certainly effective at the time.

France: 1959–64

After more than a decade of foreign-exchange crises, the French balance of payments swung into a sizeable surplus in 1959. The improvement was a direct result of the devaluation of the French franc in 1958, and also of the programme of financial reforms enacted by the new government of General Charles de Gaulle. The devaluation was probably excessive: the improvement of the balance of payments was exceptionally rapid, and by 1961 France had displaced Germany as the country with the world's biggest chronic surplus. A slow process of adjustment was, however, at work. By 1962–3, the inflationary consequences of France's strong payments position were starting to make themselves felt at home, in spite of official efforts to neutralize them, and it was being authoritatively predicted that before the end of 1964 the surplus would be completely eliminated by the rising level of demand and by higher prices (I.M.F., 1964, pp. 90–92). But this reckoned without General de Gaulle. The General did not want the surplus eliminated, for it was one of the most vital props of his foreign policy. Therefore, neither a change of the parity nor any other major switching policy that might have eased the balance of payments was employed to combat inflation in France. Instead, restrictive financial policies were applied. As a result France's balance of payments surplus was preserved, indeed even increased, but the growth of the French economy was brought to a virtual halt (I.M.F., 1965, pp. 85–8; Yeager, 1966, pp. 399–403).

France in 1959–64 provides a prime example of the clash of national interests that often manifests itself in the process of balance-of-payments adjustment. From the point of view of other countries, elimination of the French surplus was a desirable objective, since it was such a large source of disequilibrium in the international economy. From the point of view of France's president, however, the proper objective was different. General de Gaulle was involved in a political struggle to enhance French international prestige and power. His aim was to reduce outside influence in Europe – particularly United States influence – and he was prepared to use every means at his disposal. One of the most useful instruments available to him was the French balance-of-payments surplus, which by adding more than \$4.5 billion to his reserves between 1959 and 1964 enabled him to keep a steady pressure on the United States gold supply – and thereby on United States policy. This was an instrument of foreign policy which he wanted to keep.

In the early years of the surplus it was not difficult for the French authorities to implement de Gaulle's objectives, for immediately after the financial reforms of 1958 inflationary pressures were marginal in France and could be easily contained by financial policy. But as the surplus persisted, upward pressures on demand and prices were found to accumulate, just as they had in Germany after

1955 and in Canada in 1950. How was the French Government to act? Germany and Canada had acted to resist the pressures of inflation by adjusting the balance of payments. Because that course of action would have conflicted with his political objectives, de Gaulle chose to employ restrictive financial policies instead.

Early in 1963 limits on bank credit expansion were tightened. In April the authorities began controlling the prices or retail mark-ups on many manufactured consumer goods. And in September a comprehensive 'stabilization programme' was announced, including additional price controls, reduction of the Government's budget deficit, cutbacks of Treasury loans to enterprises, and a further tightening of credit restrictions. The results were striking. Demand and price inflation were halted, but so too was the real growth of the French economy. After a half decade of steady expansion, gross output levelled off in the first quarter of 1964 and then stagnated. In fact, it was not until the second quarter of 1965 that any signs of recovery became visible. That was the price France paid for the preservation of its balance-of-payments surplus.

Balance-of-Payments Deficits

The policy problem posed for a country in deficit is precisely the opposite of that just illustrated for three countries in surplus: it is what to do about the internal *deflationary* impact of an excess of payments over receipts. But the problem of deficit is even more serious than the problem of surplus, because not just one but *two* intrinsic constraints operate to compel the government to adjust. Not only is there an *internal* constraint, a limit set by institutions on the extent to which a deficit's deflationary effects can be neutralized by off-setting financial policies, but of even greater importance, there is an *external* constraint on the extent to which the deficit can be financed – namely, the limit set by the size of the country's monetary reserves plus its access to foreign credit facilities. That is why countries in deficit must usually take the first corrective measures. If a deficit persists for very long, demand and price deflation must inevitably follow, unless either the deficit is eliminated or adequate means are found for financing it. This was the common policy problem shared by Italy in 1962–5, the United Kingdom in 1964–7 and the United States in 1961–7.

Italy 1962–5

Following several years of exceptional strength, the Italian balance of payments weakened from a surplus of almost $600 million in 1961 to a near zero balance in 1962, and to a deficit of more than $1·2 billion in 1963. At the beginning of 1964 Italy was the major deficit country in the world (I.M.F., 1965, pp. 88–9). The Italian authorities reacted to the foreign-exchange crisis in the classic manner of the gold-standard era, first financing the deficit, then deflating the domestic economy by means of restrictive monetary and fiscal policies. The response of the balance of payments to these adjustment policies was also classic: exports increased, imports declined, and by 1965 Italy was again a major surplus country (Modigliani and La Malfa, 1967; I.M.F., 1964 and 1965).

The Italian experience in 1962–5 was virtually a textbook case – one of those comparatively rare instances of serious disequilibrium when one policy instrument alone happens to be enough to achieve the two policy objectives of internal and external balance. The deterioration of the Italian balance of payments after 1961 resulted from an overheating of the domestic economy, specifically from an excessively rapid expansion of incomes and spending inside Italy. Payments deficit coincided with demand inflation. The Government chose to apply a policy of demand deflation – and the remedy proved effective. In the course of 1964 the balance of payments improved and the economy cooled off. Unfortunately, the Government overshot its mark: the balance of payments not only improved, it shifted into substantial surplus; and the economy not only cooled off, it ended up in recession.[4]

Before 1961, the level of unemployment (and under-employment) in Italian agriculture had been comparatively high. Consequently, wages and prices had tended to rise rather slowly in Italy, lending strength to the balance of payments by encouraging exports and by retarding the rate of growth of imports. But by 1962 the market for skilled and semi-skilled labour was becoming tight, partly because of migration to other countries and partly because of Italy's own rapid rate of economic expansion. Unions therefore began to exert pressure on employers, wages began to rise far in excess of productivity, and domestic expenditures began to accelerate. As a result, the trade balance weakened steadily throughout 1962 and 1963.

To deal with this situation, the Italian authorities initiated a programme of restrictive monetary and fiscal policies. Devaluation of the lira was ruled out on the grounds that it would be an inappropriate response to a disturbance caused by current inflation; and the same reasoning lay behind the rejection of other more selective switching policies as well. Direct expenditure-reduction seemed to be most suited to the nature of the disequilibrium. Therefore, monetary policy was progressively tightened, beginning in May 1963, and later in the year this action was supplemented by a series of contractionary fiscal measures, including special new sales taxes, reductions of government expenditures, and price and rent controls. These adjustment measures were expected to take effect over a period of months. In the meantime, the government hoped to finance the deficit by continuing to sell spot exchange out of its own

4. Some economists have argued that it was *necessary* for the Government to 'overshoot the mark'. According to this point of view, Italy was suffering from an 'inflationary psychosis': before stability could be restored, that psychosis had to be destroyed by a really sharp deflation. Evidence for this point of view is seen in the fact that after 1965 the Italian economy successfully maintained both internal and external balance on a continuing basis.

reserves, as it had been doing from the beginning of the crisis.

Regrettably, before the effects of the adjustment measures could be felt, Italy's ability to finance the deficit was strained to the utmost by a sudden and enormous outflow of capital during the winter of 1963-4. A political crisis had broken, inspiring fears that the authorities might yet be forced to devalue. The lira was subjected to severe selling pressures: in the first quarter of 1964 alone, the over-all payments deficit approached $500 million. The authorities actually lost more than $600 million of their reserves. Devaluation was avoided only by the co-operative efforts of several of the world's major financial powers, who in March arranged for a credit package totalling approximately $1 billion to help Italy support the lira in the exchange market (Coombes, 1964). In addition, the Government drew $225 million from the International Monetary Fund. These steps immediately broke the speculative wave. As market confidence in the lira revived, and as Italy's restrictive financial policies took hold, the balance of payments quickly strengthened – though, as indicated, the improvement was unfortunately overdone, as was the restriction of domestic expenditure. In 1965 the payment surplus swelled to almost $1·6 billion, while employment declined and the real rate of growth of the economy was cut in half. The adjustment policies were effective; they may also have been somewhat excessive.

United Kingdom: 1964–7

The history of Britain's post-war economy is written in a long and dismal series of crises of the balance of payments (Rolfe, 1966, chapter 5; Yeager, 1966, chapter 21). Each of these crises was serious, and all were interesting to students of balance-of-payments policy. Any one might have been chosen for the illustrative purposes of this chapter. However, only the prolonged crisis of 1964–7 will be discussed in detail here. This episode is singularly important because it turned out to be a watershed for British policymakers.

For the first time in almost a generation, combined adjustment policies of expenditure-reduction and selective expenditure-switching proved insufficient to eliminate a payments deficit, and in the end a more general switching policy also became necessary. Thus it was that on 18 November 1967 the pound sterling was devalued from $2·80 to $2·40. This was the second devaluation of the post-war period and the first since September 1949.[5]

A problem as chronic as that of the U.K balance of payments is undeniably difficult to diagnose and cure. Several alternative explanations of the imbalance are possible. Analysis begins with the fact that Britain seems unable to earn on a regular basis sufficient foreign exchange from its ordinary commercial transactions to finance the net outflow of private long-term capital plus special government payments for military and foreign-assistance purposes. In a sense, therefore, one could say that 'the core of Britain's payments weakness is an inadequate export performance' (Hirsch, 1965, p. 29). But in another sense one could as easily say that the 'extremely heavy' long-term investments and official payments are the 'true nub' of the problem (Manser, 1966). And in a third sense one could say that neither is at fault – rather, that the real culprit is the short-term capital account. Britain, as banker of the sterling area, maintains a dangerously small ratio of monetary reserves to liquid liabilities. When reserves decline, confidence in sterling wanes, and a purely *banking* drain tends to develop. Short-term capital outflows do not add to the U.K. deficit, as officially defined (see chapter 1), but they do add to the pressures on British reserves. From this point of view, the U.K. balance of payments is weak fundamentally because of the sterling balances (Cadman, 1967).

Thus diagnosis in the British case is difficult. Certainly it is true that runs on the sterling bank have tended to develop whenever the balance of payments has shown signs

5. A running commentary on the 1964–7 crisis is given in Coombes (1965) and subsequent half-yearly additions to this series.

of deteriorating on either current or long-term capital account. And certainly it is also true that the current and long-term capital accounts have tended to deteriorate with depressing regularity. Following a run on sterling in 1947 and devaluation in 1949, sterling crises have recurred in 1951, 1955, 1956, 1957 and 1961 as well as 1964–7 (Hirsch, 1965, pp. 47–9). In part these continual pressures on sterling have resulted from structural changes in the world economy and in the economy of the United Kingdom, and are a reflection of Britain's decline from the centre of a complementary imperial network of markets and sources of supply to the status of just one industrial nation among many. However, in part too they have resulted from a significant cost-price disparity favouring Britain's chief commercial rivals in Europe and Japan – a disparity which, between crises, has frequently been aggravated by current inflation of the British economy. This inflation has occurred not only as a consequence of the 'cost-pushing' of British labour unions (which tend to demand wage increases far in excess of productivity growth), but also as a by-product of the British Government's traditional reliance on so-called 'stop–go' policies to deal with the recurrent deficits in the balance of payments.

Throughout the 1950s and early 1960s, whenever a deficit emerged, the Government reacted with adjustment policies designed mainly to reduce rather than to switch expenditures. Economic growth would be 'stopped' by deflationary monetary and fiscal policies. Then, when the crisis was past, a 'go' period would ensue as financial policies were eased. Economic growth could resume and employment would be permitted to rise, leading eventually to cost and price inflation as incomes and spending expanded. Soon conditions would be generated for a new balance-of-payments crisis. Now 'stop' policies would be adopted, but instead of cost and price deflation, mainly unemployment would result. The cycle would be complete, and the adverse cost-price disparity would be aggravated.

The last complete 'stop–go' cycle followed the exchange

crisis of 1961, during which 'stop' policies had left a half million workers unemployed. The Government began to reflate the economy in late 1961 and 1962. By 1963 inflationary pressures were again becoming apparent, and by early 1964 the British economy was booming. By the same token, the current account was deteriorating seriously, and so was the deficit on long-term capital account. In response to these adverse developments, monetary policy was tightened as early as February, 1964. Fiscal policy, however, remained easy, mainly because of the impending national election scheduled for October, which made the Conservative government reluctant to raise taxes or cut public spending. Consequently, the over-all payments deficit widened steadily, and speculation on devaluation began to mount. In September and October the pound was hit by repeated and increasingly forceful waves of selling – by pure speculators, by merchant speculators, even by investors desiring to hedge their sterling assets. Selling was heavy in both the spot and forward exchange markets, the former sales adding directly to U.K. reserve losses, the latter sales adding indirectly by opening up an intrinsic discount on sterling. By the time the Labour party was elected to office on 15 October, Britain was facing a balance-of-payments crisis more grave than any since 1949.

In 1949 the Government, then also controlled by the Labour party, had ended the crisis by actually devaluing the pound. In 1964 the Labour Party was loath to repeat itself, even though a devaluation that year could easily have been blamed on past Tory ineptitude; Labour just did not want to be known as 'the party of devaluation'. And so devaluation was ruled out. Devaluation would not work, it was asserted, either because it would start an unending spiral of domestic inflation or because all other important countries would follow with devaluations of their own. Furthermore, devaluation would be an abnegation of Britain's world responsibilities, and might perhaps even spell the end of the sterling area. Besides, devaluation would be immoral, since it would mean repudiating

Britain's obligations to foreign holders of sterling balances, and would also profit speculators at the public's expense.

There is not space here for a detailed evaluation of Labour's case against devaluation in 1964. It is enough to say that given the complexity of the British balance-of-payments problem, a strong case might have been made either way (Conan, 1966, chapter 3; Hirsch, 1965, chapter 3). In any event, since devaluation was ruled out, some alternative course of action was required. The Government decided on a return to 'stop–go', combining mild expenditure-reduction with some selective expenditure-switching policies. On 26 October an emergency surcharge of 15 per cent (later reduced to 10 per cent) was imposed on all imports except foods, tobacco and basic raw materials. In addition, duties on fuels were raised and partial rebates of indirect taxes were introduced as an export incentive. And on 11 November the Labour Government's first budget instituted higher taxes and a reorganization of the corporate tax structure designed to reduce the outflow of long-term capital.

Unfortunately, these adjustment measures were not enough to convince the market that devaluation was out of the question. As in Italy, the previous winter, fears were rampant that the authorities might yet be forced to alter parity. Throughout November sales of sterling accelerated, and on 24 November, the day after Bank Rate was raised to the crisis level of 7 per cent, a virtual avalanche of selling occurred. Indeed, speculators almost won their gamble then and there. It was clear that the British authorities could not much longer continue to finance the deficit at the current rate: their gold and dollar reserves were practically exhausted, and they were heavily committed in the forward market as well. However, on 25 November the central banks of eleven countries together with the Bank for International Settlements came to the Government's rescue with a credit package totalling $3 billion – three times the sum provided for Italy just eight months earlier and supplemented a week later by a $1 billion drawing from the International Monetary Fund. For the time being, the $2·80 parity of sterling was safe.

But it was not safe for long. Sterling never did recover to a position of strength like that attained by the lira after the Italian rescue operation. Over the next three years short-lived periods of buoyancy for the pound were to alternate regularly with much longer periods of pressure and crisis. Time and again speculators attacked (or fled from) the $2·80 parity, convinced that it could not be long maintained, and each time the parity was defended by official intervention in both spot and forward markets, with international co-operation ensuring Britain of adequate means to finance the payments deficit. Meanwhile, the Government was continually trying to supplement the combined expenditure-reducing and selective expenditure-switching policies first applied in the autumn of 1964 with additional adjustment measures. In April 1965 restrictions on foreign travel and capital exports were tightened, steps were taken to reduce the Government's budget deficit, and a 'voluntary' incomes policy was introduced. Two months later further cut-backs in intended Government expenditures were announced, and legislation was passed for a new 'selective employment tax'. (The S.E.T., a wage tax on all employment offset by greater rebates to manufacturing industries, was intended to increase the relative profitability of export-type enterprises.) Finally, a year after that, a truly massive attempt was made to 'stop' the economy: a comprehensive austerity programme was proclaimed, freezing wages, increasing taxes, reducing travel allowances, and further cutting public spending both at home and abroad. Of course, throughout the entire period monetary policy remained restrictive.

Yet, in spite of these deflationary financial policies, the balance of payments stubbornly refused to improve, and indeed tended to deteriorate easily in the face of such events as the British seamen's strike in the spring of 1966 and the Middle East War of June 1967. By late September 1967, when a dock strike began in Britain, the Government's position seemed untenable. 'Stop–go' had failed: expenditure-reducing and selective expenditure-switching policies had been unable to cure the deficit, and massive international credits and co-operation would be unable to continue financing it. British reserves and external credit facilities were virtually exhausted, the current and long-term capital accounts were again deteriorating (the trade deficit in October was the largest ever recorded), and speculators were once more selling heavily in the spot and forward markets. The Government had little choice. After three years, Labour was compelled to devalue after all. Parity was reduced by 14·3 per cent – enough, it was hoped, to reverse the speculative outflow and eventually also to improve the trade balance. Significantly, no other major country followed with a devaluation of its own (although more than two dozen smaller nations did devalue along with sterling). It is regrettable that when this was written it was still too soon to estimate the effectiveness of the devaluation as a final solution to this latest crisis of the British balance of payments.

United States: 1961–7

Although the United States balance of payments had been in deficit every year, with one exception, since 1950, it was not until about 1958 that the persistent dollar outflow from America became a cause of much concern to policy makers.[6] The years before 1958 were the years of the so-called 'dollar shortage', when the outflow of dollars – averaging roughly $1·5 billion a year – was actually welcomed by the rest of the world as a means of replenishing depleted national reserves. But in 1958 the deficit swelled to $3·5 billion, and then to almost $4 billion in 1959 and again in 1960. By the time the Kennedy Administration

---

6. The one exception was 1957, the year following the first Suez crisis, when U.S. exports were temporarily inflated by petroleum sales to Europe. Numerous writers have reviewed the U.S. balance of payments problem. Among the best discussions are Aubrey, 1964; Hansen, 1965; Rolfe, 1966, chapter 6; Yeager, 1966, chapter 25.

came into office in January 1961, it seemed obvious that the era of the dollar shortage had ended and that in its place a new era of 'dollar glut' had begun. It would no longer be sufficient merely to *finance* the deficit; the balance of payments would now have to be *adjusted*. Since 1961 the U.S. Government has initiated a variety of measures to stem the dollar outflow. Nearly all have been designed to switch expenditures selectively rather than to switch them generally (devaluation) or to reduce them (deflation); the contrast with the Italian and British examples is striking. It is striking also that at the end of 1967 the American balance-of-payments problem was still as serious as ever – if not more so.

It is interesting to consider the causes of the American payments problem. At times, the disturbance has clearly been monetary in origin. During the period 1958–60, for example, the United States was suffering from an adverse cost-price disparity *vis-à-vis* continental Western Europe and Japan, resulting partly from excessive European devaluations in 1949, and partly from excessive American wage inflation in the early and middle 1950s (Machlup, 1965b, pp. 44–8). However, this situation did not last long, for already in the early 1960s the disparity of costs and prices was speedily being eradicated by an expansion of demand in Europe and Japan far more rapid than that in the United States. Between 1958 and 1964 America was less inflationary than any other major industrial country (Machlup, 1965b, p. 37). But this situation did not last long. After 1964, American costs and prices began to inflate again, as spending for the war in Vietnam was increased. By 1967, a significant disparity seemed once more to be developing.

Monetary factors thus contributed substantially to the American balance-of-payments problem, at least during 1958–60 and after 1964. But monetary factors do not provide a complete explanation; structural factors were also at work. In fact, the real international economic position of the United States has been seriously hurt by a number of important structural developments in the post-war world economy. Demand and supply schedules have been shifted adversely by, for instance, the growth of foreign capacity and the elimination of bottlenecks since the end of the Second World War; by improvements in foreign technology which have tended to reduce the American lead in industrial applications; by increases of U.S. consumer receptivity to imports; and by the formation of the Common Market, the European Free Trade Area and other regional groups (Lary, 1963, chapter 3). Moreover, these shifts have been reinforced by, and have also induced, parallel changes in the pattern and rate of private international capital movements. Since 1956, and especially after 1960, long-term capital exports from the United States have been enormous. Short-term capital exports have occasionally been in the same position, particularly during periods when fears of devaluation or exchange controls have been aroused. And as if all these factors were not enough, the U.S. Government itself has assumed a responsibility to lend and spend abroad immense sums for foreign aid and military purposes.

Despite all these adverse monetary and structural developments, some prominent American economists have denied that the payments deficit is a serious problem (Despres, Kindleberger and Salant, 1966). The deficit is said to be desirable because it permits the United States to perform a vital role as financial intermediary between foreign (especially European) lenders who prefer liquidity and foreign (especially European) borrowers who prefer to extend their liabilities into the future. This is a unique structural explanation of the dollar deficit. It is derived from the debt structure of America's international investment position: the fact that the United States is a creditor long-term and a debtor short-term (see chapter 1) is taken as proof that the country intermediates between foreign lenders and borrowers by lending long and borrowing short – that is, by running a balance-of-payments deficit according to standard accounting procedures. This may be a *deficit* – it *is* a decline of the net liquidity position of the

United States – but it is presumably no *disequilibrium,* any more than a bank is in disequilibrium when it makes loans and enters deposits in its books. This is only a trade of liquidity, profitable to both sides and hence serving to promote important cosmopolitan economic objectives. It follows that the proper objective of American balance-of-payments policy should be to preserve the deficit, not to eliminate it.

However, preservation of the deficit as an objective of American policy presupposes that America's creditors would be willing to accumulate dollar balances indefinitely – and this they have been increasingly reluctant to do since as far back as 1958–60. This means that the American Government has had no choice but to treat the deficit as a real adjustment problem to be solved: balance (or close to it), not deficit on the order of magnitude of recent years, has had to be the country's principal external goal.[7]

Superficially, the American problem appears very similar to the British. Like Britain, America seems unable to earn from its ordinary commercial transactions enough to finance the net outflow of private and public capital. Moreover, like the pound, the dollar is subject to purely banking drains whenever confidence in parity is shaken. By analogy, therefore, some economists have argued that the Americans should try to use the same sorts of adjustment policies as the British have employed – namely, either deflation or devaluation. But analogies of this kind have so far been resisted by the U.S. Government.

7. In fact, the United States has been rather ambiguous in defining its external policy objective (other than insisting that the deficit must be reduced); this is partly because of disagreements regarding the proper measure of balance (see chapter 1). At times, the authorities seem to imply that they would be satisfied with a deficit held to a range of approximately $1–1·5 billion a year – that is, to just about the amount by which America added to world reserves during the era of the dollar shortage. At other times, the authorities seem to be aiming for zero balance. And at yet other times, particularly when antagonisms against America's European creditors are running highest, the goal seems actually to be surplus.

Deflation has been resisted by the American Government basically for one reason: the balance of payments represents a very small part of U.S. economic activity. Britain needs to trade to survive, America does not. America is a continental power, virtually self-sufficient, with a foreign sector which is relatively insignificant in terms of the over-all domestic economy. Very large changes of national income are therefore required to have any noticeable effect on the country's external position. It is not surprising that Americans are reluctant to reduce local expenditures solely to adjust the balance of payments – 'to let the tail wag the dog', as it is so often phrased. Besides, as previously indicated, the United States has not been a conspicuously over-heated economy (as Italy was in 1961–3), except since 1965. During the half decade or more before that, domestic spending grew less rapidly than in any other major industrial country (except Britain). For the most part over the course of the American payments problem, the aggregate level of domestic spending has not been regulated specifically with the aim of eliminating the external deficit. The main emphasis of policy has been, rather, on switching devices – though not on devaluation.

Devaluation has been resisted by the American Government for two main reasons. Firstly, the authorities have stressed the predominant position of the United States as an international trader. Britain could devalue in 1967 and only some smaller countries followed with devaluations of their own. But America could not devalue, it is feared, without all of the other important countries following as well. America's competitive strength is already too much a matter of concern to foreign governments. In addition, the authorities have stressed the predominant position of the dollar as an international currency. The pound serves as a reserve currency for just a limited group of countries, the dollar serves the entire world. When the pound is devalued, the structure of the sterling area only is affected. But should the dollar be devalued – whether other currencies follow or not – the structure of all of international finance

would be affected, since the fixed-price relationship between the dollar and gold is the linch-pin of the Bretton
Woods exchange system. The U.S. authorities believe that
the dollar–gold price relationship must be kept just as it is
if international monetary chaos is to be avoided.

With both deflation and devaluation ruled out, the only
alternative left to the American Government has been to
switch expenditures selectively, while attempting to finance
the deficit for its duration. A variety of financing mechanisms have been devised to avoid direct drains on the U.S.
gold reserve. Starting in 1961, European governments
were encouraged to use their dollar accruals either to pre-
pay long-term debt obligations to the United States, or to
invest in special medium-term securities denominated in
their own currencies (the so-called 'Roosa bonds') rather
than to convert into gold. In addition, the authorities began
to intervene actively to support the dollar in both the spot
and forward-exchange markets, using foreign currencies
made available through a newly created network of re-
ciprocal intergovernmental credit arrangements ('swaps');[8]
to encourage co-operative efforts in supporting the price
of gold in private markets (the 'gold pool'); and to draw
on the facilities of the International Monetary Fund.

In seeking to switch expenditures selectively, the Americans focused their policies initially on the current account
rather than on the capital account. Immediately after taking
office, the Kennedy Administration began to tie foreign-aid
loans and grants to the purchase of American products, as
well as to favour American producers over foreign producers
on military contracts overseas. In addition, new export-
financing facilities were created, and programmes of export
and foreign tourist promotion were initiated. And, finally,
wage-price 'guideposts' were issued in the hope of prevent-
ing a cost-push inflation in the United States – a kind of rudi-
mentary incomes policy.

Unfortunately, these measures were inadequate. Before

8. Before 1961, the U.S. authorities supported the price of the dollar
in just one way – by selling and buying gold.

long, it became clear that policy-makers would have to broaden their focus to encompass the capital account as well; indeed, the capital account soon became their prime focus. At first, their only effort aimed at influencing financial flows had been 'Operation Twist'. Starting in 1961, short-term interest rates had been held high in order to attract inflows of interest-sensitive international capital, while long-term rates were held low in order to encourage a faster rate of growth at home. However, the effort to 'twist' the interest-rate structure met with only limited success. In 1963 it was supplemented by the 'Interest Equalization Tax', a measure designed to cut back certain types of portfolio investment abroad, and in 1964 long-term rates themselves were permitted to start moving upward. In February 1965 a comprehensive programme of 'voluntary' restraints on all forms of capital outflow was instituted.

Operation Twist was an effort to approach both internal and external balance by means of a 'mix' of expenditure policies – specifically, by a mix of the separate components of monetary policy. It was succeeded by a more orthodox fiscal-monetary mix after 1963, once all components of monetary policy – long-term as well as short-term – were paired with the external-balance objective, since all along fiscal policy had been paired with the internal-balance objective. As early as 1962 an investment tax credit had been enacted to stimulate the domestic economy. In 1964 taxes on corporate and personal incomes were lowered generally, for the same reason. Regrettably, the fiscal-monetary mix broke down after 1965. Domestically, it proved more difficult to raise taxes than to lower them, even after it became obvious to everyone that spending on the Vietnam War was dangerously overheating the economy at home. Internationally, it proved difficult to prevent other governments, mainly those in Europe, from raising their interest rates *pari passu* with U.S. rates, since European governments prefer to pair monetary policy with the objective of internal rather than external balance (and at this time they were fighting inflation). In 1967 the U.S. balance of payments deteriorated badly and toward the end of the year, following sterling's devaluation, the dollar was subjected to intensive waves of speculative selling. On New Year's Day 1968, the Government announced new mandatory restrictions on capital exports together with a package of other selective switching devices. Some time must pass before it will be possible to estimate the effectiveness of these latest adjustment policies.

References

ALEXANDER, S. S. (1951), 'Devaluation versus import restrictions as an instrument for improving foreign trade balance', *International Monetary Fund Staff Papers*, vol. 1, pp. 379–96.

ALIBER, R. Z. (1962), 'Counter-speculation and the forward exchange market: a comment', *Journal of Political Economy*, vol. 70, pp. 609–13.

ALIBER, R. Z. (1963), 'More about counter-speculation in the forward exchange market', *Journal of Political Economy*, vol. 71, pp. 589–90.

AUBREY, H. G. (1964), *The Dollar in World Affairs: An Essay in International Financial Policy*, Frederick A. Praeger for the Council on Foreign Relations.

BALANCE OF PAYMENTS STATISTICS REVIEW COMMITTEE, (1965), *The Balance of Payments Statistics of the United States*.

BANK OF ENGLAND (1964), 'The balance of payments: methods of presentation', *Bank of England Quarterly Bulletin*, vol. 4, pp. 276–86.

BERNSTEIN, E. M. (1956), 'Strategic factors in balance-of-payments adjustment', *International Monetary Fund Staff Papers*, vol. 5, pp. 152–9.

BINHAMMER, H. H. (1964), 'Canada's foreign exchange problems: a review', *Kyklos*, vol. 17.

CADMAN, J. R. (1967), 'Sterling, the U.K. and Europe', *Westminster Bank Review*, February, pp. 31–43.

COHEN, B. J. (1966), 'Adjustment costs and the distribution of new reserves', *Studies in International Finance*, no. 18, Princeton, International Finance Section.

CONAN, A. R. (1966), *The Problem of Sterling*, St Martin's Press.

COOMBES, C. A. (1964), 'Treasury and Federal Reserve foreign exchange operations', *Federal Reserve Bank of New York Monthly Review*, vol. 46, pp. 167–8.

COOMBES, C. A. (1965), 'Treasury and Federal Reserve foreign exchange operations', *Federal Reserve Bank of New York Monthly Review*, vol. 47.

COOPER, R. N. (1964), 'Dollar deficits and postwar economic growth', *Review of Economics and Statistics*, vol. 46, pp. 155–9.

COOPER, R. N. (1966), 'The balance of payments in review', *Journal of Political Economy*, vol. 74, pp. 385–94.

COOPER, R. N. (1968), *The Economics of Interdependence: Economic*

Policy in the Atlantic Community, McGraw-Hill for the Council on Foreign Relations.

DESPRES, E., KINDLEBERGER, C. P., and SALANT, W. S. (1966), 'The dollar and world liquidity: a minority view', *Economist*, February 5.

EINZIG, P. (1964), *The Euro-Dollar System*, St Martin's Press.

EINZIG, P. (1966), *A Textbook on Foreign Exchange*, St Martin's Press.

ELLSWORTH, P. T. (1964), *The International Economy*, third edition, Macmillan, New York.

FELLNER, W. *et al.* (1966), *Maintaining and Restoring Balance in International Payments*, Princeton University Press.

FLEMING, J. M. (1968), 'Guidelines for balance-of-payments adjustment under the par-value system', *Essays in International Finance*, no. 67, Princeton, International Finance Section.

GOLDSTEIN, H. N. (1966), 'Further thoughts on official support of the forward exchange rate', *Quarterly Journal of Economics*, vol. 80, pp. 443–55.

GRUBEL, H. G. (1966), *Forward Exchange, Speculation, and the International Flow of Capital*, Stanford University Press.

HABERLER, G. (1966), 'Adjustment, employment and growth', in W. Fellner *et al.*, *Maintaining and Restoring Balance in International Payments*, Princeton University Press, chapter 6.

HANSEN, A. H. (1965), *The Dollar and the International Monetary System*, McGraw-Hill.

HARROD, R. (1966), 'The speed of adjustment', in W. Fellner *et al.*, *Maintaining and Restoring Balance in International Payments*, Princeton University Press, chapter 7.

HELLER, W. W. (1967), *New Dimensions of Political Economy*, Norton.

HIRSCH, F. (1965), *The Pound Sterling: A Polemic*, Gollancz.

HØST-MADSEN, P. (1962), 'Asymmetries between balance of payments surpluses and deficits', *International Monetary Fund Staff Papers*, vol. 9, pp. 182–99.

I.M.F. (1964), *Annual Report*, International Monetary Fund.

I.M.F. (1965), *Annual Report*, International Monetary Fund.

JOHNSON, H. G. (1961), 'Towards a general theory of the balance of payments', in *International Trade and Economic Growth: Studies in Pure Theory*, Harvard University Press. Reprinted in 1968 in *Readings in International Economics*, Richard D. Irwin. [Page references relate to this edition.]

JOHNSON, H. G. (1964), 'Economic nationalism in Canadian policy', *Lloyds Bank Review*, October, pp. 25–7.

JOHNSON, H. G. (1966), 'The objectives of economic policy and the mix of fiscal and monetary policy under fixed exchange rates', in W. Fellner *et al.*, *Maintaining and Restoring Balance in International Payments*, Princeton University Press, chapter 8.

KENEN, P. B. (1964), 'Measuring the United States balance of payments', *Review of Economics and Statistics*, vol. 46, pp. 139–44.

KENEN, P. B. (1966), 'Financing and adjustment: the carrot and the stick', in W. Fellner *et al.*, *Maintaining and Restoring Balance in International Payments*, Princeton University Press, chapter 9.

KINDLEBERGER, C. P. (1963), *International Economics*, third edition, Richard D. Irwin.

KINDLEBERGER, C. P. (1965a), 'Balance-of-payments deficits and the international market for liquidity', *Essays in International Finance*, no. 46, Princeton, International Finance Section.

KINDLEBERGER, C. P. (1965b) ,'Germany's persistent balance-of-payments disequilibrium', in R. E. Baldwin *et al.*, *Trade, Growth and the Balance of Payments, Essays in Honor of Gottfried Haberler*, Rand McNally and Co., pp. 230–48.

LAMFALUSSY, A. (1966), 'Limitations of monetary and fiscal policy', in W. Fellner *et al.*, *Maintaining and Restoring Balance in International Payments*, Princeton University Press, chapter 10.

LARY, H. B. (1963), *Problems of the United States as World Trader and Banker*, National Bureau of Economic Research, chapter 1 and appendix A.

LEDERER, W. (1963), 'The balance on foreign transactions: problems of definition and measurement', *Special Papers in International Economics*, no. 5, Princeton, International Finance Section.

MACHLUP, F. (1950), 'Three concepts of the balance of payments and the so-called dollar shortage', *Economic Journal*, vol. 60, pp. 46–68.

MACHLUP, F. (1958), 'Equilibrium and disequilibrium: misplaced concreteness and disguised politics', *Economic Journal*, vol. 68, pp. 1–24. Reprinted in F. Machlup, *International Payments, Debts and Gold: Collected Essays*, Scribners, 1964, p. 119, 128–32. [Page references relate to this edition.]

MACHLUP, F. (1965a), 'Adjustment, compensatory correction, and financing of imbalances in international payments', in R. E. Baldwin *et al.*, *Trade, Growth and the Balance of Payments, Essays in Honor of Gottfried Haberler*, Rand McNally, pp. 185–213.

MACHLUP, F. (1965b), *Involuntary Foreign Lending*, Wicksell Lectures 1965, Almqvist and Wiksell, Stockholm.

MACHLUP, F. (1966a), 'In search of guides for policy', in W. Fellner *et al.*, *Maintaining and Restoring Balance in International Payments*, Princeton University Press, chapter 3.

MACHLUP, F. (1966b), 'The need for monetary reserves', *Banca Nazionale del Lavoro Quarterly Review*, no. 78, pp. 199–201.

MANSER, W. A. P. (1966), 'The U.K. balance of payments – a bar to the European Community?', *Westminster Bank Review*, November, p. 14.

MEADE, J. E. (1951), *The Theory of International Economic Policy*, vol. 1: *The Balance of Payments*, Oxford University Press, New York.

MODIGLIANI, F., and LA MALFA, G. (1967), 'Inflation, balance of payments deficit and their cure through monetary policy: the Italian example', *Banca Nazionale del Lavoro Quarterly Review*, no. 80, pp. 3–47.

MUNDELL, R. A. (1960), 'The monetary dynamics of international adjustment under fixed and flexible exchange rates', *Quarterly Journal of Economics*, vol. 74, pp. 249–50. Reprinted in R. A. Mundell, *International Economics*, Macmillan, New York, 1968, chapter 11.

MUNDELL, R. A. (1962), 'The appropriate use of monetary and fiscal policy for internal and external stability', *International Monetary Fund Staff Papers*, vol. 9, pp. 70–79. Reprinted in R. A. Mundell, *International Economics*, Macmillan, New York, 1968, chapter 16.

MUNDELL, R. A. (1968a), *International Economics*, Macmillan, New York.

MUNDELL, R. A. (1968b), 'The redundancy problem', in R. A. Mundell and A. K. Swoboda (editors), *Monetary Problems in the International Economy*, University of Chicago Press.

NIEHANS, J. (1966), 'Wage and price guideposts in the context of balance-of-payments adjustment', in W. Fellner *et al.*, *Maintaining and Restoring Balance in International Payments*, Princeton University Press, chapter 13.

NURKSE, R. (1945), 'Conditions of international monetary equilibrium', *Essays in International Finance*, no. 4, Princeton, International Finance Section. Reprinted in 1949 in *Readings in the Theory of International Trade*, Blakiston.

NURKSE, R. (1956), 'The relation between home investment and external balance in the light of British experience, 1945–1955', *Review of Economics and Statistics*, vol. 38, pp. 121–54.

O.E.C.D. (1966), *The Balance of Payments Adjustment Process, A Report by Working Party No. 3 of the Economic Policy Committee of the O.E.C.D.*

ROBINSON, J. (1947), 'The foreign exchanges', *Essays in the Theory of Employment*, second edition, Blackwell. Reprinted in 1949 in *Readings in the Theory of International Trade*, Blakiston. [Page reference relates to this edition.]

ROLFE, S. E. (1966), *Gold and World Power: The Dollar, the Pound, and Plans for Reform*, Harper and Row.

SCAMMELL, W. M. (1961), *International Monetary Policy*, second edition, St Martin's Press.

SCITOVSKY, T. (1965), 'Requirements of an international reserve system', *Essays in International Finance*, no. 49, Princeton, International Finance Section.

SCITOVSKY, T. (1966a), 'Alternative methods of restoring balance', in W. Fellner *et al.*, *Maintaining and Restoring Balance in International Payments*, Princeton University Press, pp. 198-9.

SCITOVSKY, T. (1966b), 'A new approach to international liquidity,' *American Economic Review*, vol. 56.

SCOTT, I. O., and SCHMIDT, W. S. (1964), 'Imported inflation and monetary policy', *Banca Nazionale del Lavoro Quarterly Review*, no. 71, pp. 390–403.

SMITH, J. S. (1967), 'Asymmetries and errors in reported balance of payments statistics', *International Monetary Fund Staff Papers*, vol. 14, pp. 211–36.

SOHMEN, E. (1966), *The Theory of Forward Exchange*, Studies in International Finance, No. 17, Princeton, International Finance Section.

STEIN, H. (1965), 'The evolving international monetary system and domestic economic policy', *American Economic Review Papers and Proceedings*, vol. 55, p. 204.

SWAN, T. (1963), 'Longer-run problems of the balance of payments' in H. W. Arndt and M. W. Corden (editors), *The Australian Economy: a Volume of Readings*, Cheshire Press, pp. 384–95. Reprinted in 1968 in *Readings in International Economics*, Richard D. Irwin.

TINBERGEN, J. (1952), *On the Theory of Economic Policy*, North-Holland Publishing Company.

TOBIN, J. (1966), 'Adjustment responsibilities of surplus and deficit countries', in W. Fellner *et al.*, *Maintaining and Restoring Balance in International Payments*, Princeton University Press, chapter 16.

WONNACOTT, P. (1965), *The Canadian Dollar, 1948–1962*, University of Toronto Press.

YEAGER, L. B. (1966), *International Monetary Relations*, Harper and Row.

Index

163